INTRODUCTION TO THE SERIES

This series of books is intended to inform and assist those of you who are in the beginning stages of starting a new small business venture or who are considering such an undertaking.

It is because you are confident of your abilities that you are taking this step. These books will provide additional information and support along the way.

Not every new business will succeed. The more information you have about budgeting, cash flow management, accounts receivables, marketing and employee management, the better prepared you will be for the inevitable pitfalls.

A unique feature of the Crisp Small Business & Entrepreneurship Series is the personal involvement exercises, which give you many opportunities to immediately apply the concepts presented to your own business.

In each book in the series, these exercises take the form of "Your Turn", a checklist to confirm your understanding of the concept just presented and "Ask Yourself", a series of chapter-ending questions, designed to evaluate your overall understanding or commitment.

In addition, numerous case studies are included, and each book is cross-referenced to others in the series and to other publications.

BOOKS IN THE SERIES

► **Avoiding Mistakes in Your Small Business**
David Karlson, Ph.D.

► **Budgeting for a Small Business**
Terry Dickey

► **Building Teams for Your Small Business**
Robert B. Maddux

► **Buying a Business: Tips for the First-Time Buyer**
Ronald J. McGregor

► **Buying Your First Franchise: The Least You Need to Know**
Rebecca Luhn, Ph.D.

► **Extending Credit and Collecting Cash**
Lynn Harrison

► **The Female Entrepreneur**
Connie Sitterly

► **Financial Basics of Small Business Success**
James O. Gill

► **Getting a Business Loan: Your Step-By-Step Guide**
Orlando J. Antonini

► **Great Customer Service for Your Small Business**
Richard F. Gerson

PERSONNEL MANAGEMENT
FOR THE
SMALL BUSINESS

by Neville C. Tompkins

THE
CRISP
SMALL BUSINESS &
ENTREPRENEURSHIP
SERIES

CREDITS

Editor: Janis Paris

Layout/Design: ExecuStaff

Cover Design: Barry Littmann

Library of Congress 95-83115
ISBN-1-56052-363-8

CONTENTS

CONTENTS (continued)

CONTENTS (continued)

PREFACE

This book offers a broad survey of the personnel management field and crystallizes the author's experiences in helping small businesses establish the basics of a personnel management program.

For the small business manager the book raises questions about the type of personnel function desired, the role of personnel management in the small business, and the services that can be provided by a full- or part-time activity. For the personnel professional entering a small-business environment, it is intended to be a road map of professional items to consider as the position evolves.

CHAPTER ONE

WHAT

IS

PERSONNEL

MANAGEMENT?

PERSONNEL MANAGE-MENT

In some companies it is called personnel management. In other organizations it is the human resources department or the employee relations function. A few companies still label the activity "industrial relations." Some small organizations lump personnel management activities under the broad umbrella of "administration," believing that functions such as personnel, accounting, and scheduling are staff or administrative functions—established to help the company be successful.

Whatever designation is applied to the personnel management activity, it is a "staff" function there to help the "line" organization perform its main job of providing a product or service. The words *personnel management, human resources,* and *employee relations* are used interchangeably in this book.

Each of the chapters in this book deals with matters a small-business manager should consider when implementing a program of personnel or human resources management. For newly appointed personnel professionals, the book can act as a road map of human resource practices to include in a basic personnel management program.

Personnel management activities in small business tend to be informal, and few items are committed to written format or policies. That may work fine but over time, as we will see, a more formal structure of personnel management is helpful to business success.

In small business the personnel function often consists of one person, full- or part-time—a personnel assistant or clerk—reporting to an administrative manager who has broad staff responsibilities. As companies grow, a personnel manager or human resources director may be added, assisted by one or more professionals or assistants, depending on the size of the company and perceived need for personnel management services.

THE LINE AND STAFF RELATIONSHIP

Line managers are those managers and supervisors directly responsible for manufacturing or selling a product or providing a service. These are the plant managers, the production superintendents, the shift supervisors, the sales managers, and sales representatives who are at the heart of the business organization.

Development of the personnel management function in business has been evolutionary. As businesses grew busy, line managers were no longer able to handle every detail inherent in their jobs. They had to reach out for staff assistance, from persons who would help them or offer expertise in carrying out their main responsibilities.

Thus, we saw the growth of the finance and control function to account for the income and expenses of the business, the development of a quality-control department to monitor quality levels in the product and to inform line managers almost by the minute of variances in quality. Other functions such as industrial engineering, planning, and scheduling evolved to assist busy line managers with details they could no longer give their attention to.

So, too, with the personnel function. Even in small organizations some line supervisors and managers still perform functions normally associated with the personnel management activity—trying to do the interviewing and hiring, attempting to focus on improved wages and benefits, stumbling through a review of policies, often after the company has been cited by a government agency.

Line managers found as organizations grew that they had to delegate some of these functions—for instance, asking the personnel representative to prepare an advertisement and conduct initial interviewing, presenting several candidates to the manager for final selection.

A busy line manager doesn't usually have the time, patience, or expertise to carefully check out wage rates in the local labor market. With a personnel manager in place, the competitiveness of wage rates and benefits are researched and recommendations made to line management for improvements.

Line managers still have the responsibility to discipline employees under their direction but often a personnel manager will provide guidance for the most effective handling of the discipline and offer input on any federal or state laws that might affect dealing with the infraction.

While line managers focus on day-to-day problems they often look to the personnel expert to recommend policies on employee issues such as methods of combating use of drugs in the workplace or occupational health problems caused by materials or chemicals used in the production process.

DETERMINING THE ROLE

What role is the personnel professional expected to play in the small organization? The critical starting point is to find out what management expects from the personnel person. The best human resources managers find out right at the start what their clients require and then strive to meet those needs.

In a client-focused approach, the personnel professional determines what the business and its key members expect from the function, rather than working from any preconceived ideas. A meaningful program on human resource management must also be shaped by the organization's philosophies, culture, policies, and procedures.

Once the personnel professional knows and understands those needs, it's a good technique to develop a plan in writing that includes goals, an order of priority, and a timetable to implement those goals. Then the human resources person should review the plan with management and get agreement on it. An example of a personnel management plan and priorities for a growing small business is shown in Chapter 10.

A number of surveys has been conducted on what executive management seeks in its human resource function. Perhaps the best known of these is the annual survey jointly conducted since 1985 by the Society for Human Resource Management and CCH, Inc., the human resource information services publisher. The 1995 survey showed that firms who use the best HR practices have higher productivity and higher market performance relative to their competitors.

THE NONSPECTACULAR ROLE

The personnel management function does not bask in the glory of achieving new production records, landing a new sales contract, or designing machinery that will increase production and improve quality. Personnel management activities are less glamorous than that.

Many activities in the personnel function especially in small businesses, involve paperwork and face-to-face interaction with managers and employees—separating opinions from facts, mastering detail, studying trends, reviewing laws, listening to complaints, and investigating cases.

What comes next is where the personnel professional gains stature—or fails to—by aligning facts and research and recommending changes and assisting various levels of management to implement the recommendations. The meaty part of the function involves persuasion and salesmanship.

Personnel people have customers, or clients—the managers, supervisors, and employees who draw on services from the personnel department. Some of these requests come automatically—the need to hire new employees, information about benefit plan coverages, or the dozens of "what do I do about?" questions that come the way of the personnel office.

Successful personnel professionals are those who listen to their clients, discovering what their needs are and adjusting or developing services to meet client needs. To establish credibility it's important to get feedback from everyone you deal with.

COSTS VS SAVINGS

Providing a formal personnel management service to an organization does not come without cost. There is the salary of one or more full- or part-time persons, the cost of insurance and medical benefits, and the other costs per employee of vacations, holidays, unemployment insurance, and workers' compensation coverage. A cost-conscious business will also figure in the cost of workspace, telephone service, and the many small items required to make a business activity operational. Adding one or more persons to the payroll costs money.

But a viable human resources function should be paying its way through competent assistance to the line organization. Without staff assistance line managers become overloaded with detail which detracts from their role in the business—producing a product or providing a service at a profit. An effective personnel management service provides a professional service that causes line managers to look on the personnel function as a "partner" in the business.

How successful the personnel person and services are will be measured to a large degree by the satisfaction of its clients—the departments for which it provides service. It will be measured by the adding of real value—that is, services those clients could not provide as well as can the human resources staff.

It's important for a person embarking in a human resources role at a small business to understand the different but interdependent roles of line and staff departments. The human resources people (who fulfill a staff function) are there to assist line managers in making their jobs more effective.

Take the case of a New Jersey metal stamping company. The sole plant supervisor of this 70-person shop prides himself on the effective orientation and induction of new employees to safe work practices. New hires report on a Monday morning and the orientation and induction task takes nearly a full morning—at a time when the supervisor's efforts and experiences should be focused on getting the plant off to a good start for the workweek.

The personnel coordinator at the facility has offered to assist with the orientation but the supervisor has declined. The supervisor's efforts to ensure a good orientation for new employees are commendable, but in this example we have a line supervisor overloaded at a critical time of the workweek.

An effective compromise would be to have the plant supervisor say a few words of introduction to the new employees then wind up the orientation with an opportunity for questions, wishes of good luck on the job, and discussion of safe work practices. Most of the material in-between could be handled effectively by the personnel coordinator and departmental trainers.

A Profit Orientation

A good personnel function costs money to establish but should help improve profitability by

- ► Helping to hire more qualified employees

- ► Decreasing costs by reducing employment-related problems

- ► Enhancing the motivation of present employees to work smarter

- ► Providing guidance in areas of management that line managers do not possess

All of these points are considerations for the managers of a small business seeking to initiate a professional personnel program.

ASK YOURSELF

► How can the personnel professional best determine the role he/she is to play?

► How do personnel professionals pay their way in an organization?

► At this point, does a full-time or part-time HR person make more sense for your business?

CHAPTER
TWO

IMPLEMENTING PERSONNEL MANAGEMENT

CHAPTER TWO

GETTING STARTED

How does a personnel management activity get started in a small organization? Usually, it is in response to a need.

The need for a personnel person may develop from an expansion of the business—the need to hire more employees with one person focused on the recruiting and training of new staff. Sometimes federal or state laws dictate the need for a person to coordinate compliance—perhaps the requirements of the federal law on drug-free workplaces or the need to conduct medical examinations of persons who must wear respirators on the job. Meeting the myriad of employment-related laws is often the basis for the start of a formalized human resources function in a company.

In a small business, it may be the more mundane need to organize employee personnel files in a better manner because of supervisors' inability to track the work records of their employees. Good personnel files are basic to an effective personnel activity.

SCOPE OF THE FUNCTION

The personnel management function in organizations, small and large, takes on many sizes and shapes, most often tailored to the needs of the particular organization. This is a basic but very important decision for a business manager: "What do I need?" and "What do I want?"

Often the configuration of the personnel function is governed by the following considerations:

► What level of personnel management is needed to assist the line organization in running the business? Is it a full- or part-time need, clerical or professional, or should the activity be outsourced—that is, provided by nonemployee outsiders?

► What federal, state, and locals laws and regulations impact this company and industry and what assistance, if any, does the line organization require in complying with those employment-related laws and regulations?

- ▶ What help can a personnel professional offer in the recruitment and selection of new staff and coordinating the transfer and promotion of present staff?

- ▶ What basic records are needed—employee personnel files, employee medical records, insurance, pension—to run the business effectively and meet requirements of government laws?

- ▶ What will determine the company's policies on wages, salaries, and benefits? Does the company plan to be competitive in the local labor market and/or competitive in the industry in which it operates?

- ▶ How does management want to deal with employees—a cooperative manager-employee work environment or allow the employees to drift towards unionization?

- ▶ How will the business communicate with its employees—through supervisor-to-employee contact or will they supplement that basic communication with other media?

- ▶ If the company is in an expanding mode, what training activities should be undertaken with supervisors and employees? What awareness training should be mounted to acquaint managers with provisions of new federal and state laws that affect the business?

- ▶ In many working environments safety and the occupational health of workers may be at risk because of the nature of the manufacturing, construction, or service process. What safeguards should be applied and what safety activities should be implemented to protect workers and keep control of workers compensation costs?

THE SHRM SURVEY

A 1994 survey by the Society for Human Resource Management (SHRM) identified 55 activities that one or more personnel/human resource departments were found to perform. The principal functions included:

- Benefits
- Compensation
- Employment
- Human resource information systems
- Internal communication
- Labor relations
- Legal issues/compliance
- Organization development and planning
- Performance management
- Recruitment
- Research
- Training
- Wage and salary administration

A number of other functions are sometimes lumped into the domain of personnel—facility security, employee activities and recreation programs, wellness and health promotion programs, and fitness centers.

The multiple roles of the personnel professional will be dealt with in subsequent chapters of this book. A key question for a small business owner to answer at this point is: Do I want to formalize a personnel management position on a part-time or full-time basis? That decision will dictate the size and scope of the function, cost of the operation, and relative level of service to the organization.

In small companies the personnel professional is a generalist—a jack-of-all-trades in the personnel field, handling a multitude of responsibilities, problems, and concerns. As the business grows other specialists such as recruiters, benefits professionals, and perhaps a training manager may be added.

When a personnel function is established formally in a small business, the function may be delegated to an administrative manager to oversee, with clerical employees asked to pick up bits and pieces of the personnel responsibility.

In other cases a competent employee who has demonstrated success in other assignments with the organization may be promoted to fill and carry out the function. Or, if full-time coverage is desired, a person with experience in personnel management may be hired to organize and manage the function.

Your Turn

In your most recent business experience, indicate the following:

► Is my HR need at the generalist level, or is it time to hire specialists?

WHAT'S INVOLVED?

How does such a person get the personnel function launched? Here are some suggestions for the basics:

► What activities and services does the company want the personnel person to perform? List the most important functions desired and then develop a set of goals and designate the time required to achieve those goals. (A sample approach is suggested in Chapter 10.)

► Become familiar with federal and state employment laws which affect the company and industry. The nearest state department of labor (listed under "State" in the blue pages of the telephone book) and the federal department of labor (listed under "United States" in the telephone book) can provide copies of laws that affect the business. Some copies are available without charge; others may be obtained at cost.

► Meet your managers and your employees. Understand their needs, their concerns, and their view of the business organization. Walk the plant or facility. Be available.

► Federal and state laws change frequently. The personnel person should attend a basic employment law seminar to learn the fundamentals of those laws, then attend an annual update program on laws. Ignorance of the law can cost employers dearly.

► Subscribe to a human resource information service or newsletter to keep informed about regulation changes.

► The personnel professional should join the local human resources professional group to network about ideas, concerns, and sources of additional help. Membership will offer the opportunity to meet other personnel professionals working in nearby organizations, many of whom face the same problems and challenges as the newly appointed personnel person.

Outsourcing: The Use of Independent Contractors

Some companies choose not to have a personnel person on staff but prefer to have the function performed on a full- or part-time basis by outside consultants or independent contractors. These nonemployees come in when and as needed to carry out the personnel function or are available by telephone to answer questions from managers. These are not usually full-time persons so total costs to the company for the service may be less.

A note of caution should be introduced at this point about classifying workers as independent contractors. An employer can save money on social security contributions, fringe benefits, and other expenses when an employee is correctly classified as an independent contractor. But if the consultant is incorrectly classified as an independent contractor, the employer may be liable for federal and state payroll taxes, underpaid minimum wages, overtime, contributions to an employee benefit plan, and fines and penalties.

A written agreement clearly spelling out the contract terms is an important start to show that the person is an independent contractor, not an employee. Details on whether an individual is an independent contractor or employee are available from the Internal Revenue Service. Ask for their publication #15.

DESIRABLE QUALITIES

Personnel professionals come from many educational and work backgrounds. Some are administrative or clerical personnel in small organizations who advance to the human resources position. Others are manufacturing or accounting staff who, for an assortment of reasons, are asked to lead the personnel function.

Sometimes personnel people are picked for the job because they like people or somebody in management likes them and wants to give them a break. Sometimes it is a dumping ground for persons who haven't done well in other functions but who have long service with the company.

There are a number of qualities that make for a successful personnel professional. The list may seem long but there is a lot of common sense in these qualities—they are characteristics that would make the person a good manager or professional in *any* profession.

The desired qualities for a personnel professional are:

- ▶ A person who knows the subject matter of personnel administration and human resources management and is regarded as being knowledgeable and expert in the field.

- ▶ A person with credibility. Personnel professions have to establish themselves as honest and responsible employees, the starting point to earning the trust of management and employees.

- ▶ A person who maintains confidentiality of information.

- ▶ A team player who shows commitment to departmental and company goals. Personnel professionals who work well with others are recognized as cooperative.

- ▶ A person who has the interactive and consulting skills to assist others, think through problems, and arrive at some solutions that are good for the business and fair to employees.

► A change agent who has the ability to say "no" when the request is illegal or contrary to organizational policies.

► A person who is positive and optimistic. Moaners and groaners tend to lower morale and good morale is essential to a successful working environment.

► A person who is willing to stand up for what is right. In turn, there is nothing wrong in saying "I don't know" and then checking to find the missing information.

► A person who has a mindset to stay abreast of developments in business and the personnel profession. It is also a person who is able to provide accurate, up-to-date information on developing trends in business and employment-related laws affecting business.

The Role of Spokesperson

While the personnel person works for management, a true personnel professional is often regarded as a spokesperson for both management and employees. At times it is a balancing act.

As a management representative the personnel professional is expected to explain the needs of the business and the reasonable and lawful actions of management to employees and reaffirm those policies for some employees who may not want to adhere to company policies and procedures.

In turn, a more motivated workforce is one where employees can speak up about their concerns to a sympathetic ear. That good listener *should be* a line manager but *may often be* the personnel person who is able to carry the concerns of employees to management and gain a change in procedures. Or, in unusual circumstances, it may involve arranging for special consideration for an individual employee.

Administrative and Project Work

Experts in the field often divide the personnel function into two distinct aspects—the administrative aspect and the more challenging project aspect of the work.

Administrative items are the basics of personnel work— putting a new hire on the payroll, processing benefits claims for employees, or investigating a discrepancy in an employee's paycheck. Many of these items are routine, though they appear big to the person seeking a solution. These administrative areas cannot be ignored if credibility is to be maintained and an adversarial relationship avoided.

The project aspects of the personnel function are the fun parts of the job—initiatives such as developing an improved attendance policy, recommending a new human resource information system, or assisting with the establishment of a Total Quality Management (TQM) program. These are the meaty aspects of the job and the personnel professional should welcome these opportunities to improve the profit- ability of the business as positive steps in professional development.

HR BUDGETS AND STAFFS

How much money should be budgeted for a personnel management function, and what should the ratio of HR staff be to total employees? That will obviously vary with management's determination of the services required and the nature and complexity of the business.

But some comparisons can be helpful. The Bureau of National Affairs, Inc., and the Society for Human Resource Manage- ment (see Appendix V for more information) have conducted a number of surveys over the years to determine the size and extent of these services. Here are some interesting statistics from the 1995 survey, responded to by 407 organizations:

▶ The median HR staff is 1.6 staff members for every 100 employees among organizations with fewer than 250 workers, compared with 0.5 for facilities with 2,500 or more employees.

► Employee per-capita expenditures for a personnel activity varied but a median expenditure of $792 per employee was recognized, with a variance from $55 to $7,362 per employee. In companies with fewer than 250 employees an average of $1,519 was budgeted for 1995.

► Human resource specialists are on staff in about half of the responding companies. Thirty percent of all surveyed employers have at least one benefit specialist on the HR department staff. Specialization within HR is particularly common among hospitals, schools, and other "nonbusiness" organizations, as well as in larger companies.

► HR expenditures relative to operating costs represent a median of 1.1 percent of total budgeted operating costs, unchanged from the previous year.

GAINING FEEDBACK

There are a large number of persons within the organization and outside of it with whom the personnel person must interact on a regular basis and who can provide feedback on the effectiveness of the personnel function's efforts.

Within the organization there is senior management and descending levels of management down to first-line supervisors. The personnel person also has major contact with workers—the employee group. A variety of personnel services touches each and every person, for one reason or another, within the organization.

Outside of the company there is contact with regulatory agencies, vendors, applicants, and retirees and their families who need to be considered as the program evolves.

How effective the personnel professional is in these contacts will dictate the long-term success of the function.

Line managers are measured on how they decrease costs, improve efficiency, expand productivity, and improve profitability. There are comparable opportunities for the personnel professional to talk the same language as the line manager: How can compensation plans be shown to improve motivation and loyalty to the business? How can benefits help the organization be competitive in the local labor market? How can safety training reaffirm the need for safe work practices and reduce accidents?

The progressive personnel professional will listen to clients and contacts and direct energies to key business concerns.

The Outlook

The growth in organizational stature of the personnel management activity will depend on the skills brought to the function by those occupying the position in the small organization. If these professionals earn recognition and appreciation from other departments, they will be able to function effectively, contribute to the organization's profitability, and create a healthier environment for everyone.

ASK YOURSELF

▶ How can you determine what kind of job you're doing?

▶ What are the disadvantages of using an outside "contract" person for the personnel function?

▶ What are the three most pressing personnel issues that need attention in your business?

CHAPTER THREE

HIRING
CONCERNS

RECRUIT AND SELECT EMPLOYEES

"Find us some people" may be a first assignment for a new personnel person.

In a newly established personnel department, one person may be asked to coordinate the recruitment, selection, and testing of applicants for jobs in the facility. The person may be called the employment manager or recruiter.

Recruiting assistance to line and staff managers is one of the most visible parts of personnel management—and prompt, effective action in this area can win applause for the personnel professional. Presenting a panel of final candidates to the hiring manager is not the end: An effective personnel professional will also help managers in choosing the best candidate for the job.

The size and scope of the recruiting function will be dictated by a number of business elements—the size and hiring mode of the business, employee turnover in the organization, and the number of specialty disciplines such as engineers and scientists in the company. The tightness in a local labor market can also be a factor in generating hiring activity.

Numerous federal, state, and local laws impact the recruitment, selection, and hiring activity and prohibit discriminatory practices in hiring. Highlights of federal regulations on employment-related laws are outlined in Appendix II. This chapter cross-references some of these laws and also outlines a number of management considerations in developing a selection and hiring process.

Ignorance of the law is not accepted as an excuse. An applicant, an employee, or a former employee may file a charge for any infraction of a law; it is the employer's responsibility to demonstrate innocence in its employment practices. Personnel professionals need to know what they are doing in this sensitive and potentially costly area.

THE COST OF HIRING

Businesses are becoming increasingly more aware of the costs (See Appendix III for additional information and formulas) of adding new persons to the payroll—costs that were not even closely looked at less than a decade ago.

Line and staff managers need to be reminded about the costs (1995) of adding a single new hire to the payroll:

Social Security and Medicare

Employers must match employee contributions; that is, 6.2 percent of a worker's income (up to $61,200 a year) for Social Security and another 1.45 percent for Medicare.

Federal and State Unemployment Taxes

At the federal level this is 0.8 percent of payroll on the first $7,000 of income, and state unemployment taxes range from 1.2 percent to 10 percent on a variety of income bases.

Disability Insurance

Some states have mandatory disability insurance, carved out of the typical employer-provided benefits package, and employers are mandated to contribute to these funds.

Workers' Compensation Insurance

This varies with the state and the nature of the business and ranges from 1 percent to as much as 20 percent of the worker's income level.

Vacation, Holiday, and Sick-leave Pay

Some states legislate minimum vacation allowances. While holiday and sick-leave pay are not legally required, these programs allow an employer to be competitive for workers in the local marketplace.

Medical and Dental Insurance

Although not legally required in most states, the strain of competitiveness for employees in some areas encourages the offering of coverage.

Pensions and Profit Sharing

Again, this is not legally required, but may be necessary to be competitive.

Overhead Costs

Here, companies prorate the expense of floor space, workstation, telephone, computer, and share of heat and electricity.

EMPLOYMENT APPLICATIONS

The employment application form is a very important document—it starts the applicant assessment process.

An employment application form should be designed to elicit maximum information about the applicant's qualifications and work experience as they relate to the particular employment needs of the business. A carefully developed application form should be able to respond positively to this query: "Does each question on the form seek information that is job related?"

Borrowing an employment application from a neighboring company may seem like an easy way to create an application form by simply reprinting the form with a company name at the top. But be cautious. Some questions on the borrowed form may be illegal and the questions posed may not suit your needs. And if you buy a stock employment application form from a printer or a forms distributor, carefully review each question for legal acceptability. That's your company's responsibility.

The final draft of an employment application form should be reviewed for nondiscriminatory language by an experienced human resources professional and an employment law attorney.

An application form should require the applicant's signature, attesting that the information provided is accurate. Persons who submit a resume in response to a job opening should also be required, if they are being seriously considered for employment, to complete and sign the company's application form which should elicit additional information beyond the resume, some of which may not be entirely favorable to the candidate—but very necessary for the employer's evaluation of the applicant.

Remember that resumes are a self-marketing tool for applicants. They are designed to show the applicant in his or her best light—and not to detract from the candidacy with any negatives. Signing the "Authorization" section of the application will remind the applicant that falsification of information is normally grounds for termination.

A single application form may not fit all needs so some companies have developed several application formats—a short version for factory openings, another for office work, and still others for technical, professional, and managerial vacancies.

Keeping Employment Application Forms Up-to-Date and Legal

Employment laws at the federal and state level change frequently. Forward-thinking companies make annual reviews of the questions asked of applicants to be sure the information solicited is in compliance with these evolving laws.

Persons who work with the recruiting process regularly— employment managers, recruiters and personnel assistants— should be asked for input to changes.

A good application form should develop maximum information about an applicant, within legal parameters, before an interview takes place.

Reviewing the Equal Employment Opportunity Commission (EEOC) guidelines on selection standards is also a good step to be sure that any revisions to the application form are in compliance with those guidelines. The official name of that publication is "Uniform Guidelines on Employee Selection Procedures" issued in 1978.

An in-depth review of the interviewing guidelines under the Americans with Disabilities Act (ADA) will assist with revisions to the application form. Also presented are interviewing questions that comply with ADA, the legal role of employment medical examinations, checking of information on the applicant's disabilities, and the like.

A revised application form should indicate an effective date on the bottom of the cover page. Copies of any superseded application forms should be destroyed.

Your Turn

▶ Does each question on your employment application form ask for information that is job related?

Substance Abuse

Substance abuse screening is becoming more prevalent as employers try to weed out potential problems of drug abuse before a person is hired. Some companies put a notation at the top of their employment application form: "The employer may require satisfactory passing of a urine test for substance abuse before employment commences." Further, many employers print in the release or disclaimer section above the area for the applicant signature wording such as "the applicant agrees to take a substance abuse screening test at a laboratory designated by the company."

Applications and Resumes: How Truthful?

Getting at the real truth of an applicant's education and work experience presents challenges and problems for personnel professionals. The *challenge* is to verify job-related information about an applicant so that a fair evaluation may be made of all candidates and a job offer made to the most qualified applicant. The *problem* is that some applicants make untruthful statements about themselves or show work experience or education that never occurred. Former employers are reluctant to give out much information on their former employees for fear of defamation suits.

In most organizations, lying on a employment application form or making material omissions, is grounds for termination, and persons have been discharged or dropped from the selection process for telling untruths on such an important document. Among newly hired employees, where background checks or other procedures reveal lies or failure to meet job-related standards, an immediate review of the situation should be made and, where cause is established, the employee should be terminated.

Verification of an applicant's background takes time, effort, and some determination to get the full—and, hopefully—true story on a person's background. Verification is imperative in some customer-contact and public-service jobs because the employer could later face a charge of negligent hiring if the checking is not done carefully and well documented.

CHECKING REFERENCES

The importance of checking references of prospective employees cannot be overemphasized. Employers have a right to know who they are hiring and that statements made on the employment application form and resume are accurate.

The reference checking process is made more difficult these days because of the reluctance of many companies to give out information due to risks of defamation law suits. These companies limit their information-giving to dates of employment and position(s) held—and little more. Requiring an applicant to execute a signed release can prompt a former employer to release more than just the basics.

Checking of references can be time-consuming but is a necessary part of the candidate evaluation process. This section offers some suggestions.

Check out the verifiable facts and statistics with the candidate's former employer. Do not mark comments on the employment application itself but keep a separate record showing the information received or information the employer was not able to confirm.

Personnel offices of former employers are not likely to know much detail of the employee's work performance so the personnel representative may want to talk to former supervisors. Where possible, check verifiable information with these former supervisors, keeping questions to job-related information.

For some candidates background checking may include investigating driving records, checking for criminal convictions, academic credentials, and business references. Professional agencies can handle this type of work for the employer and protect the company from receiving improper information about a candidate. If a credit reporting agency is used, be sure to advise the applicant in advance.

Where applicants have been presented by an executive search firm, the "head hunter" should do initial reference checking, subject to overview by the prospective employer.

If discrepancies are encountered with final candidates, present the information to the applicant, asking for his or her side of the story. Some people have perfectly explainable reasons for job gaps or other incomplete information on an application form.

And if important information provided on the application and resume cannot be matched through reference checking, the employer just may want to bypass that particular applicant.

Progressive human resource managers know the importance of investigating job applicants. They have methodical approaches to reference checking that help the employer's defense of any potential discrimination or legal claim.

NEGLIGENT HIRING

Employers are properly cautious about giving out information on former employees for fear of a defamation suit by the ex-employee, alleging that "false and malicious" information was given out. Balanced against this concern, however, is the opposing need to be protected from a lawsuit for negligent hiring—which could face an employer if information was not provided to a specific question.

Defamation is typically charged when slanderous or libelous statements harm the reputation or professional credibility of another person.

Some states recognize the basis for legal action for negligent hiring when an employer fails to conduct a reasonable investigation of work, education, and personal statements—any information that shows an unacceptable level of risk. Employment representatives must ensure that the reference check is sufficiently thorough and well documented to resist any claim of negligent hiring.

RECRUITMENT SOURCES

There are many traditional and time-tested ways to find employees, including:

► Internal candidates, where a transfer or promotion is involved

► "Walk-ins" to the company's offices or facility

► Posting a sign on the property "Now Interviewing"

► Newspaper and radio advertisements or postings to an electronic job service

► The state job service

► Employment agencies that charge the employer a fee if their candidates are hired

► Former employees with good work records

► Referral of applicants by present employees

► Agencies assisting the disabled

► Persons affected by downsizing

► Job fairs

- ▶ For professional and managerial jobs, national publications and professional journals

- ▶ Using contingent workers—persons from temporary agencies

- ▶ Placement offices of colleges or trade schools

- ▶ College students available for part-time or summer work assignments

- ▶ Outsourcing the recruiting function to independent contractors

- ▶ Student interns

- ▶ For certain trade jobs, union hiring halls

These are the typical avenues to source new employees. There are other less conventional ways—interviewing persons who are on welfare and want to work, persons completing government-sponsored training programs, persons being released after serving prison terms, or immigrants who have authorization to work in the United States.

As an example, state job services are often overlooked. Some recruiters have established successful contacts with these government-funded job placement agencies. That strong relationship is more than a telephone contact—an effective working relationship involves visiting the job service professional at the local office to discuss job needs. Many companies invite the job service specialist to tour their facility so that the placement officer has a better understanding of the needs of the employer. Close interaction with the local Job Service office can pay off in excellent referrals.

And remember that any advertising or bulletin board announcements seeking applicants must meet government regulations on nondiscrimination. In developing advertising avoid discriminatory language that refers to race, sex, age, or a person's religious affiliation or national origin. Use gender-neutral terms such as "food-server" instead of waitress, "sales representative," instead of salesman. It is a good practice to add to the bottom of the employment advertisement "EEO employer M/F, individuals with disabilities, Veterans/Disabled Veterans."

Over time one or more of these recruitment methods will turn out to be productive for certain types of applicants. Effective recruiting means fine-tuning productive sources of applicants and setting aside other avenues.

In this electronic era, resumes can be forwarded electronically or faxed directly to a company. Increasingly employers are able to match their employment needs with resumes provided by on-line computer services, reducing recruitment costs and selection time. Computerization also allows for special software to arrange an applicant tracking system, which is helpful (and sometimes required) of companies that do business with the federal government.

QUALITIES OF SUCCESSFUL APPLICANTS

Some hiring managers want to review every resume and every response to an employment advertisement. But most often it is the recruiter's task to present a selection of final candidates to the hiring manager.

The final candidates should possess the following qualifications:

► Have an educational and/or work background—the knowledge, skills, and abilities (KSA)—that closely parallel the job specifications. A written job description listing essential functions of the open position is a real help to a recruiter.

► Have career ambitions for which the opening is the next logical step; or, in the case of a lateral move, a job transfer that will provide new experiences at the same level of responsibility.

- Be currently employed or have been downsized or outplaced for legitimate business reasons.

- Show a stable work record, provide specific explanations of work history and job responsibilities, and have no unexplainable gaps in their employment history.

- Show a salary history and objective that fit into the salary range of hire.

- Indicate willingness to work in the geographic area and be ready to commute by personal or public transportation to the job.

Not every final applicant fits neatly into this desired list, but using this type of checklist should reduce the number of candidates to those most likely to be successful.

Your Turn

- How many of the items on the desired qualities list do I tend to ignore or forget?

PERSONS WITH DISABILITIES

Interviewers need to be consciously aware of the provisions of the Americans with Disabilities Act (ADA) which has had a significant effect on employment since its inception in 1990. The Act now applies to employers with 15 or more regular employees.

Persons conducting job interviews should remember a number of key definitions in the Act, such as the definitions of "disability," "qualified individual with a disability," "major life functions," "essential functions of the job," and "reasonable accommodation," as outlined in the act.

What Is a Disability Under ADA?

Under ADA a disability is defined as a physical or mental impairment that

1. Substantially limits one or more of the major life activities of an individual,

2. The individual who has a record of such an impairment, or

3. One who is regarded as having such an impairment.

Physical and Mental Impairments

A "physical or mental impairment" is defined in the Act as:

► Any physiological disorder or condition, cosmetic disfigurement or anatomical loss affecting one or more of the following body systems: neurological, musculoskeletal, special sense organs, respiratory, including speech organs, cardiovascular, reproductive, digestive, genitourinary, hemic and lymphatic, skin and endocrine, or

► Any mental or psychological disorder such as mental retardation, organic brain syndrome, emotional or mental illness, and specific learning disabilities.

Major Life Activities

Major life activities under ADA means functions such as caring for one's self, performing manual tasks, walking, seeing, hearing, speaking, breathing, learning, and working.

Qualified Individual with a Disability

ADA defines a qualified individual with a disability as an individual with a disability who, satisfies the requisite skill, experience, and educational requirements of the employment position and who, with or without reasonable accommodation, can perform the essential functions of such position.

Essential Functions of the Job

The term "essential functions" means primary job duties that are intrinsic to the job. The term does *not* include the marginal or peripheral functions that are incidental to the performance of primary job functions.

The Equal Employment Opportunity Commission (EEOC), which has responsibility for enforcing the Act, says it will consider the employer's judgment of what those essential functions are, as well as any written job descriptions.

Reasonable Accommodation

The ADA does not provide a specific definition of reasonable accommodation but rather lists examples:

> "modifying devices, services or facilities or changing standards, criteria, practices or procedures for the purpose of providing to a particular person with a physical or mental impairment . . . the equal opportunity to participate effectively in a particular program, activity, job or other opportunity."

The term also includes:

> "Making existing facilities used by employees readily accessible to and usable by individuals with disabilities . . . job restructuring, part-time or modified work schedules, reassignment or modification of equipment or devices, appropriate adjustment or modification of examinations and training materials . . . the provision of qualified readers or interpreters and other similar accommodations."

Myths About Disabilities

Persons with disabilities are now in the mainstream of employment, and employers seeking qualified applicants should consider individuals with disabilities in the selection process.

There are some myths and realities about persons with disabilities, as explained by the President's Committee on Employment of People with Disabilities:

MYTH #1: Making job accommodations for persons with disabilities is too expensive to undertake.

REALITY: In most cases an appropriate job accommodation can be made without difficulty and at little or no cost. An accommodation may be something as simple as adding an extra lever to the fare box for a driver of a public bus who is unable to reach the box because of a disability.

Of the 436 reasonable accommodations made by Sears Roebuck and Co. between 1978 and 1992, 69 percent cost nothing, 28 percent cost less than $1,000 and 3 percent cost more than $1,000. The relatively minor costs of providing reasonable accommodation are offset by the benefits resulting from increased employment of people with disabilities, reduced dependence on Social Security, increased consumer spending by people with disabilities, and increased tax revenues.

MYTH #2: Because the ADA's definition is broad and vague, frivolous discrimination claims are being made in the name of ADA.

REALITY: The ADA's definition is intentionally open-ended. Rather than listing specific conditions, the ADA defines disability as a physical or mental impairment that substantially limits a major life activity, having a record of such impairment, or being regarded as having such an impairment. According to the EEOC, Congress chose this definition because "it would not be possible to guarantee comprehensiveness by providing a specific list of disabilities, especially because new disorders may develop in the future, as they have since the definition was first established in 1973."

MYTH #3: ADA is not increasing the number of employed individuals with disabilities.

REALITY: The ADA has played a significant role in enhancing labor force participation of persons with disabilities and in reducing dependence on government entitlement programs by helping qualified individuals obtain and retain jobs. Fifty percent of ADA charges alleging discriminatory discharge filed with the EEOC generally involve individuals who want to continue working but are being fired, they claim, because of their disability. Despite these efforts, unemployment remains a significant problem for individuals with disabilities.

Job Accommodations—Situations and Solutions

SITUATION: A greenhouse worker who is mentally retarded had difficulty staying on task and knowing when to take breaks.

SOLUTION: One-on-one training was provided by a rehabilitation agency at no cost to the employer. A tape recorder was carried that gave the employee periodic reminders to stay on task and indicated break time. A set of laminated cards for the worker to carry showed the basic lists of tasks to be completed. Cost: $50.

SITUATION: A worker with kidney disease is a senior technician in the coal industry who is responsible for preparation of samples for testing. This employee requires Continuous Ambulatory Peritoneal Dialysis (CAPD) four times daily, with one exchange occurring during working hours.

SOLUTION: Space is made available in the dispensary for the employee to perform CAPD while at work. Storage space is also provided for extra supplies to be used in case of bad weather emergencies necessitating a second exchange while at work. Cost: zero.

SITUATION: An experienced electronics equipment inspector paralyzed from the waist down needs to perform tasks related to using precision equipment and assembly inspection; he needs rapid mobility about the plant.

SOLUTION: His heavy motorized wheelchair is stored on the premises. The employee uses his lightweight chair for travel around the facility. The bins containing items to be inspected are lowered and a lap board is provided for his specification books. Cost: Less than $200.

SITUATION: Because of a severe hearing loss, a nurse is unable to monitor multiple alarms on medical equipment in the critical care unit.

SOLUTION: To continue to utilize her experience and training, the hospital transfers her to a position in the laboratory where a vibrating pager and portable TTD/TTY are used to direct her to various locations throughout the hospital. Cost: $634.

Realistic Job Previews

One of the reasons for high turnover in some companies is that too little attention is given to telling—and showing—the job for which the applicant is being considered. It's a good practice to explain details of the job but it is even better to take the employee to the work site and show the job in operation. Some companies use short videos to show actual work conditions and requirements of the job.

Providing such realistic job previews will reduce dissatisfaction and turnover. The recruiting department can assist in this role but it is also important that the department supervisor attend the recruiting interview to explain how the job is being carried out.

HIRING AND ORIENTATION

The personnel representative will soon see the need to develop a hiring and orientation procedure so that basic information about the job and the company are provided to a new employee.

The selection procedure might include the following process, with each stage taking place based on satisfactory completion of the previous step:

1. Satisfactory completion of the employment application form

2. Satisfactory initial interview with the personnel representative

3. Satisfactory interview with the hiring manager

4. Written permission from the applicant to check references at former employers. Satisfactory reference from these employers with information that correlates with what the applicant provided.

5. In some companies, a pre-employment substance abuse test

6. A job offer that includes the proposed starting date, weekly or monthly salary, description of benefits, effective date for benefit coverages and employee contributions to the cost of benefits. Job offer is conditional on passing employment medical examination.

If the job offer is to be in writing, some companies send the original letter and a copy with a self-addressed, stamped envelope. The new hire can then sign the letter, keep the original, and send a signed copy back for company files.

If the job offer is accepted then the new hire presents him- or herself for orientation as follows:

1. All necessary company forms are completed. Verification of eligibility to work in the United States should be provided on the I-9 form. Employee is given a passcard.

(After an applicant has accepted the job offer, some companies mail the packet of "new hire" paperwork to the applicant for completion before starting work. This step saves time on the employee's first day and allows the person to proceed directly to the work area.)

2. Review company information documents, including an employee handbook, if used. Be sure to cover company policies on harassment and what to do if an employee has a complaint or concern.

3. Review general company safety and security rules. Specific job or department safety rules should be reviewed by the department supervisor or job instructor.

4. Turn over new employee to the supervisor for department introductions, familiarization with the department and work area, and for job training.

These general orientation procedures should be adapted to the particular company, department, and job assignment depending on whether the employee is managerial, professional, office, plant, or field (sales or technical) staff.

A well-planned orientation process for new hires may take time and effort on the part of the personnel representative, but the process makes for a positive introduction to the company.

NEPOTISM

Companies pride themselves on having good workers and when a good employee refers a relative or friend for a job, there's the temptation to think that there is an automatic "fit." This is particularly the case in small business, which is a magnet for family members and friends of employees.

Nepotism is the employment of relatives in the same organization, a practice that has existed since the dawn of time. Employers who encourage such relationships believe it provides a family-type atmosphere in the workplace.

The major risk in employee referrals of family and friends is that good feelings may be substituted at a time when critical judgment is called for. That's why nepotism is of concern to many companies.

Nepotism, without controls, can result in a negative impact on workplace morale with a tendency of family issues to get mixed up with business matters. Allegations, real or imagined, can arise about favored treatment on the job.

Screening procedures in the personnel department and by the hiring manager for a "family or friends" referral should be the same as for all candidates. References should be checked carefully as for any other applicant.

No specific federal laws deal with nepotism or the assigning of relatives to work together or for each other (other than the potential for a charge of discrimination under Title VII). In fact, a few court cases have struck down limitations employers have placed on relatives working together or for one another.

A 1993 survey by the Society for Human Resource management (SHRM) found that most organizations "encourage and employ married couples and employees related in some other way." Comments from participants in the survey indicated that married couples and other relatives in the workplace posed few, if any, problems. Some respondents commented that having relatives within the workplace actually stimulated productivity through family competition. Of the organizations that employed married couples about 73 percent had policies prohibiting husband and wives from supervising each other.

Employers have a legitimate business interest in regulating relationships between supervisory personnel and their subordinates—to avoid conflicts of interest. Restricting such relationships may be necessary to avoid the appearance of favoritism in the workplace. Any policy developed to limit impact of nepotism should emphasize that the business does hire qualified relatives of employees, as long as the company retains the right to determine whether a conflict or potential conflict exists.

Hiring of sons and daughters of employees for summer work between school terms is widely prevalent in our country. In some respects it says "thank you" to the parent for being a good employee and allows the student-worker to accumulate money for education costs. These temporary summer opportunities are not usually considered part of the nepotism problem, although many companies will not place a student under the supervision of a relative.

The personnel professional should be aware of potential problems in hiring the teenage children of employees. The Federal Fair Labor Standards Act and many state laws dictate age limits for teenage workers, the number of hours they can work, the type of work performed, and whether the work is agriculture or nonfarm (manufacturing, construction, etc.) work. An employer should require an age certificate of persons believed to be under 18 years of age. Under federal law a child under age 14 may not work at any paid job, except for children working for their parents or as newscarriers or actors.

MEDICAL EXAMINATIONS

Many companies require medical examinations of an employee before starting work so that the new hire is not exposed to workplace conditions that would cause or aggravate a health problem for themselves or co-workers.

The Americans with Disabilities Act has specific provisions governing the conduct of employment medical examinations and return-to-work medical examinations (following an illness or injury). The ADA now applies to all employers with 15 or more regular workers and generally provides:

- ► Medical examinations of new employees may be conducted *only* after a job offer has been made, as long as they are conducted for all employees, disabled or not, for the particular work classification.

- ► Pre-employment substance abuse tests are *not* considered part of the medical examination procedure and may be conducted by the prospective employer at any stage in the recruitment process.

- Medical examinations required by an employer following absence of an employee for illness or injury *must* be job related.

- Inquiries about medical conditions *before* a job offer is made are prohibited and questions are permitted only about the ability of the applicant to perform a specific, job-related task. Once a conditional job offer has been made employers may ask disability-related questions, provided they are asked or required of all employees employed in the same job category.

- There is no requirement for an employer to generate medical files for employees but, if they are retained, they must be kept apart from regular personnel files on a confidential basis in separate, locked files.

Some states have even more restrictive provisions for employee protection than the federal ADA and these rules should be reviewed so that the employer is in compliance with *both* federal and state requirements.

Other government regulations affecting employment will be dealt with in Chapter 5.

JOB TESTING

Employers are often tempted to initiate testing procedures for new hires—some of which are entirely legal, others questionable. Embarking on a testing program requires detailed knowledge of federal, state, or local laws governing such procedures—*before* the program is implemented. Job testing tends to take place primarily in larger organizations.

Proponents of job testing say that the testing process can act as a crystal ball of sorts, predicting candidates' work behaviors, without a lot of inconclusive interviewing, and can predict the candidates' chance of success on the job. In their view this is the way to gain objective feedback before a job offer is extended.

Job testing should not be the automatic "go" or "no go" for a prospect but should be used as one tool in the selection process—in addition to the employment application form, interviews, checking of references, medical examinations, and the like.

Skills Testing

To determine whether a prospective employee has the qualifications, aptitude, strength, or physical agility to perform a particular job, some employers use paper-and-pencil tests, which the applicant completes by penciling in answers, or actual on-the job demonstrations of work such as required of a typist, a carpenter, or a fork lift driver. Proponents of skills testing say that the process allows the recruiter to narrow the number of applicants to those who are truly qualified to fill the vacancy.

Unless there is a close correlation between test scores and job performance, tests should be avoided. Employers should monitor the effect of pre-employment tests on minorities and women, and if a test is negatively impacting a protected group, the employer must validate the test by using a government-dictated mathematical formula that measures the extent of the impact.

The key proviso here is: The employer must assure that these tests are job related and not used in a discriminatory manner.

Honesty Testing

Honesty and integrity tests are professionally developed psychological tests designed to determine the integrity of test takers by measuring attitudes toward theft and propensity for theft-type behavior. These tests are particularly in favor for use with employees who handle money or merchandise.

Major suppliers of these tests say that their products comply with Equal Employment Opportunity Commission guidelines on testing and their in-house studies show no adverse impact on protected groups.

Drug and Alcohol Testing

Several federal laws require pre-employment drug testing of new hires—for example, the federal Department of Transportation requires such testing—and the Americans with Disabilities Act allows an employer to conduct pre-employment substance abuse tests at *any* stage of the recruitment process. The ADA does not protect active drug abusers but offers protection from discrimination to rehabilitated drug users or alcoholics or those who were incorrectly designated as such.

A number of state laws also permit or require employers to conduct drug and alcohol testing in specific situations. But note that some state laws protect active substance abusers.

Polygraph Testing

The Employee Polygraph Protection Act of 1988 prohibits the use of polygraph tests by private employers, except in very limited circumstances. Under certain conditions the use of polygraphs is permitted for employees suspected of workplace incidents resulting in economic loss, such as theft, embezzlement, sabotage, or injury to the employer's business.

The regulations provide most employees and prospective employees in the private sector with protections against lie-detector testing in both pre-employment settings and during the course of their employment. Federal, state, and local government employees are not covered and these employees may be tested.

The Act also permits polygraph testing of:

- ► Certain employees of certain contractors engaged in national security or defense intelligence work

- ► Applicants for jobs with private security firms

- ► Prospective or current employees of companies involved in the manufacture or distribution of legal drugs

Employers are also required to post a notice outlining employee rights and highlights of the Act.

Summary

Personnel managers who are considering using skills or psychological tests should be fully aware of government requirements on employee testing at the federal and state level. In considering a test supplier determine how long the organization has been in business and ask for copies of their validation studies for the particular tests you are considering.

PROBATIONARY PERIODS

It is customary in many organizations to require employees to work a probationary or introductory period of time before being considered a regular employee. (Note the designation "regular" rather than a "permanent" employee—which could imply that the person has the job forever.) Sometimes "probationary increases" are implemented with satisfactory completion of the probationary period.

If a company decides to have a probationary period for new hires, the following elements should be considered in the procedure:

- ▶ There is no federal law at this time governing probationary periods; review state laws to see if there are any restrictions.

- ▶ Be sure that the company's application form has an "employment-at-will" statement which allows the employer—and the employee—to terminate the relationship at any time. More on this in Chapter 5.

- ▶ Make provisions for a written review of work performance at least once during the probationary period.

- ▶ Establish probationary periods of a length that ties in with the complexity of the job, say 45 days for general factory work, and perhaps up to one year for managerial or complex technical jobs.

TURNING DOWN APPLICANTS

Not every person applying for work turns out to have the interests, qualifications, or motivation for a particular job opening. At some point in the interview and selection cycle these persons may disqualify themselves, drop out of the selection process, or simply not appear for further appointments or interviews.

Similarly, a recruiter or manager may find an applicant unsuitable for a particular opening and decide in favor of a more qualified applicant. Telling the person that they are not the most suitable applicant is a responsibility that is critical to the good name of the employer and a positive reputation in the community. How do you say "no" gracefully?

Employers are not required to explain their selection process to applicants, but some companies choose to do so. Rejecting an applicant for employment in a less-than-professional manner is where dissatisfaction can start to boil and litigation can follow.

Here are some suggestions to limit the negatives of rejecting an applicant:

► Be factual about the job during the interview cycle. Overly enthusiastic recruiters and hiring managers can generate unrealistic expectations in the minds of applicants. The rejection notice then becomes a major letdown.

► Provide prompt and considerate responses to unsuccessful applicants. No response to an applicant gets expectations raised as lack of response may be viewed as "no news is good news." Polite and thoughtful responses issued promptly will decrease the likelihood of a challenge.

► Avoid becoming involved in a discussion of the applicant's qualifications compared to the person selected. Try to stay with the statement, "We selected a person who we felt was the best fit for the opening."

► If it is a company's policy to retain applications for a period of time, say so in the rejection letter.

UNSOLICITED RESUMES

A company that is not in a hiring mode may not want to be flooded with unsolicited resumes or having persons approaching the employment office looking for work. Some organizations simply put a sign in front of the building declaring "Sorry, Not hiring at this time" and advise the state Job Service accordingly.

But what about the paperwork flow of unsolicited resumes and applicants? There is no legal requirement to respond to a resume or letter of application, although some companies do so as a matter of courtesy and community relations.

A logical step in controlling the paperwork burden is to develop a company policy declaring that unsolicited resumes and letters seeking employment will not be responded to unless they are the result of a specific job opening that has been advertised. The applications and resumes of unsuccessful applicants for such jobs will then be retained in a current file for a limited period of time, say six months, and then be discarded.

A written policy on the handling of employment applications will provide a strong measure of protection in the event of complaints and markedly reduce the amount of paperwork a personnel representative has to retain in files.

ASK YOURSELF

► Why is the employment application so important?

► What are the benefits of checking applicant references?

► What is meant by the term "employment-at-will"?

► What particular education, training, or work experience characterizes the growth of the successful manager?

► In a few words, how would subordinates characterize the managerial techniques of a successful manager?

CHAPTER FOUR

RECORD KEEPING

KEEP ACCURATE RECORDS

Having an accurate and well-organized set of personnel records is so basic to the conduct of a business that it is often targeted as an early assignment for a newly appointed personnel professional.

Line and staff managers and supervisors need to have access to accurate information to manage their employees effectively—such as presenting recommendations for merit increases, reviewing employee performance records, and scanning attendance patterns.

From a legal standpoint accurate personnel records are important to the employer for self-protection to defend claims by employees who feel they have been treated unfairly.

This chapter deals with the basic but important role of effective employment-related personnel files in a small business.

INFORMATION SYSTEMS

Computers have been a boon to personnel recordkeeping—ensuring continuing accuracy of employee information. But the key is accuracy at the point of entry. If inaccurate information is input at the start, the information will remain inaccurate. Inaccurate information on employees can shake the credibility of a personnel function.

Both the type of records included in the personnel file and the length of time records are retained are important—employers must leave paper trails documenting important aspects of the employment relationship and to meet government requirements for IRS, pension, and other purposes.

But before one piece of paper goes into a personnel file a basic question needs to be raised: Will this piece of information assist in making an employment decision? If not, then the information may not be appropriate or should be kept somewhere other than in the employee's personnel file.

Federal and state governments dictate requirements for retaining some wage and hour information, and a personnel manager should determine those exact requirements before setting up a new system.

Many basic personnel records are now computerized into human resource information systems (HRIS). Payroll ledgers, attendance records, and vacation schedules lend themselves to automated entry and recovery—in fact, any item belongs in HRIS that can be collected, stored, and retrieved and is used by an organization to manage its human resources.

A good HRIS system can collect the full spectrum of information about an employee—from the date of hiring through to a pension payment and eventually death. All intervening activities such as pay transactions, compensation changes, training and development activities, benefit coverages, performance evaluations, and career planning can be included in HRIS.

A good HRIS system will have a password control access system (which limits the type of data for each official who has access) and provides an audit trail to see who is accessing the system.

Even with computerization of many personnel record items, a basic file folder with hard copies of some information is still necessary in an active personnel department.

MAINTAINING CONFIDENTIALITY

Personnel files often contain information that many employees would not want others to see. Employers must guard the right of employees to privacy of this information to protect the company from potential liability for defamation or other claims.

Personnel managers should develop restrictions on who has access to employee personnel files—only immediate supervisors, other personnel staff, department managers and perhaps others with a clear need to know. Outsiders with a right to review these files can be government inspectors and designated union representatives.

What should not be included in the employee personnel file? Certainly medical records should be excluded, as outlined below. Some employers choose to keep discrimination charges out of the employee personnel file in a separate file; immigration department I-9 forms and garnishment orders belong in still another file so that they will not jeopardize a company's defense against a charge of discrimination.

Steps can be taken to safeguard confidential information in employee personnel files and still maintain good relations with supervisors and employees. Here are some suggestions:

▶ Determine early in the game who is allowed to have what information about employees, their wages or salaries, and other key personnel information. A written policy should be developed, even in a small organization.

▶ The correct positioning of a personnel representative's desk and visitors' chairs can, at times, help protect the confidentiality of materials the personnel representative may be working on. Some personnel staff place their desk at a right angle to a visitor's chair so that the visitor cannot see the desk surface directly.

▶ Personnel representatives should make a practice of closing a confidential file folder when a person approaches their desk. Those steps will protect confidentiality and will allow the personnel representative to give full attention to the visitor.

▶ For visitors who have no business with your business, stand-up conferences may be in order. As they approach, a personnel representative may stand up from the desk and meet them a few steps away from the work area.

▶ Efforts to breach confidentiality should not be tolerated. Personnel persons may add a friendly statement such as "I'm sorry but this is confidential information I am working on," which will usually put people gently in their place. Repeated problems should be reported to a supervisor.

A personnel professional will be respected for taking a strong stand to protect confidential aspects of their work. Most supervisors and employees realize the important role that personnel has in handling confidential information.

A disregard for confidentiality, intentional or not, can quickly make a personnel representative ineffective in the job and an unwanted person on the human resources staff. Personnel staff members have lost their jobs because of breaches of confidentiality.

Your Turn

► What is your view of the importance of confidentiality of personnel records?

Employee Access to Their Personnel Files

At least half of the states now have laws authorizing employees to inspect, copy, correct, or include explanations in their personnel files. Most states require the worker to give advance notice of a desire to review the file and are allowed to copy documents from the file.

Most state regulations exclude employee access to materials such as staff planning and organization succession documents, business development information, and expansion or closure of operations if they relate to or affect more than one employee.

Personnel Information to Outsiders

Personnel managers are often concerned about how much employee information to give to outsiders–usually that is mortgage companies or banks and loan organizations that need to confirm basic information about an employee's status and earnings. Others include prospective employers seeking to check out reference information on former employees.

Many personnel departments have a written policy that these requests be in writing on the stationery of the requesting organization; other will give out information on the telephone only to well-established local organizations and to persons they know in those organizations.

One precept is certain: Do not give out *new* information—confirm only information provided by the caller.

MEDICAL RECORDS

The Americans with Disabilities Act has specific provisions governing medical records of employees and provides that these records be kept apart from regular personnel files of employees and retained on a confidential basis in separate, locked files. There is no requirement to generate medical files for employees but, if they are kept, these rules must be followed.

ADA requires that medical information on an employee must be kept confidential and shared only with those who have a need to know—possibly a supervisor who needs the information for effective placement of a disabled employee or medical and first aid staff who need to be aware of a disability situation in case of emergency treatment.

Many businesses identify the types of information that belong in medical files, not in personnel files, as the following:

- Results of an employment medical examination

- Medical insurance claim forms of the employee

- Forms relating to workers compensation claims

- Substance abuse test results

- Voluntary medical information from an employee health program or voluntary medical examinations

- Voluntary disclosure information from the applicant regarding a disability

Some states have even more stringent provisions for employee protection than the federal ADA and these rules must be reviewed so that the employer is in compliance with *both* federal and state requirements.

RECORDS RETENTION

Most personnel offices are faced with deciding over time what to keep and what to throw out of their personnel files. A company policy on records retention will alleviate this concern.

The first step is to develop a records retention policy with specific retention periods for each of the forms or materials in a human resource department. A company's legal advisor can often assist in developing such a procedure.

Here are suggestions for developing a personnel records retention policy and procedure:

▶ Secure a copy of each company or external form used in the human resource activity. Forms such as employment applications, insurance beneficiary designation forms, medical claims, earnings records, and immigration I-9 forms should be collected and reviewed.

▶ Cross-reference each of the forms to an appropriate federal, state, or local law or regulation. Review the law to determine record keeping requirements. For example, year-end EEO-1 Employer Information Report forms completed by companies with government contracts must be retained for at least three years, plus the current year.

▶ Compare these government-required retention periods to any company retention policies and adjust the retention periods *higher* if the company requires longer retention. For example, the federal Age Discrimination in Employment Act (ADEA) requires key employee information be retained for at least three years, yet many companies retain payroll information for longer periods for pension determination.

► Set up a record destruction cycle for materials and files which are no longer required beyond the end of the retention cycle. Confidential material should be shredded rather than tossed in the trash. A good record retention system requires systematic audits at regular intervals to ensure that the company's policies on record retention and destruction are indeed being followed.

Taking the time to develop a records retention policy will give personnel professionals a sense of confidence that unnecessary material and files are being thrown out and important and valuable records are being properly retained.

ASK YOURSELF

▶ What information should *not* be included in an employee personnel file?

▶ Should employees have access to their own personnel files?

▶ Can you recall a situation in your business experience where the personnel department broke confidentiality? What was the result?

CHAPTER FIVE

LEGAL
COMPLIANCE

COMPLYING WITH LAWS

A multitude of legislation which affects employers and employees in their work relationship has been enacted at the federal, state, and local level. This chapter outlines the importance of these laws as they impact personnel management.

In most organizations it is the responsibility of the human resources department to guide management in compliance with these laws and to inform employees of regulations that affect them through notices, or, where required, by training in details of the regulation.

An outline of principal federal legislation affecting the employment relationship is included in Appendix II of this book. Personnel managers should have full copies of the acts on hand or subscribe to a human resource information service that provides basic information, plus updates as laws change or court decisions provide further interpretations of the law. Several information services are listed in Appendix V.

These laws affect the day-to-day operation of a business and the employees who work there. Personnel managers need to have a broad knowledge of these laws and how and where to obtain additional information. For example, personnel professionals need to be aware of federal and any state provisions for time off for jury duty. They also need to know the legal way to calculate overtime pay for piece-rate workers. Also, some state laws prohibit inquiry into arrest records; some states require paying nonexempt employees on a weekly basis—all considerations for the personnel professional guiding the organization in compliance with the laws.

The personnel professional should understand the coverage of the law, the enforcement agency involved, any exemptions under the law, the range of penalties and the statute of limitations for applicants (or present and former employees) to file a claim. Ignorance of the law is not an acceptable excuse to government officials. The watchword for personnel professionals should be: Keep informed on developments!

POSTING NOTICES

Many federal and state laws require employers to post notices to employees about provisions of a particular law. Posters should be prominently displayed on at least one facility notice board covering matters such as the well-known EEO poster, the minimum wage posting, the yellow OSHA safety and health poster, the legally required notice to employees about workers' compensation coverages, and the poster outlining details of the federal Family and Medical Leave Act.

Notice boards can get cluttered but these are legally required postings that the personnel manager should see are in place. Failure to comply with posting requirements can result in fines and further investigations by government inspectors.

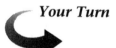

Your Turn

► Am I in compliance with government and OSHA posting requirements?

EMPLOYMENT AT WILL

Very simply, employment at will means that an employee is not bound to stay with the employer forever and the employer may terminate the employee at any time. Under this common law theory the employer has the right to hire, fire, demote, and promote whomever they choose for any reason unless there is a contract (like a labor agreement), federal, state, or local law or company policy to the contrary. At this time some 40 federal statutes put limitations on management's rights to employ at will.

Top management needs to understand the concept of employment at will and management rights and responsibilities under this doctrine. The employee application form and company handbooks should reaffirm that employment in the company is "at will." Supervisors should be trained not to use language with subordinates that suggests employment is secure for any specified period of time. The term "permanent employee" should be dropped from the vocabulary in favor of terms such as "regular employee," "temporary worker," or "part-time employee."

A terminated employee may allege an "implied contract"—that is, a real or implied promise that the job was "permanent" and not subject to discontinuance. Employees sometimes challenge this concept if the company has taken retaliatory action against them for refusing to engage in what they perceive as illegal activities.

But how terminations are handled can undermine basic employer power in employment at will. An effective personnel administrator needs to "manage" the termination process so that discrimination claims are minimized.

No Retaliation

A number of federal and state laws provide that an employer may not take retaliatory personnel actions against an employee who discloses or threatens to disclose an employer's policy or practice that violates a particular law or presents substantial danger to public health and safety. Many federal safety regulations, for example, contain "no retaliation" provisions. Most state workers compensation statutes also prohibit retaliation against persons who file workers' compensation claims or testify on behalf of claimants.

Managers and supervisors should be fully aware of the no-retaliation provisions of many laws. Lack of knowledge can cost. A personnel professional should develop awareness training sessions for line managers. Inappropriate action by a supervisor can result in charges, fines, and unfavorable publicity for the employer.

STATE-LEVEL LAWS

Most states have enacted laws covering employment-related matters and employee safety and health on the job. Some state laws almost duplicate the federal provisions but personnel managers need to become *very* familiar with state laws affecting their businesses as *many of the state laws provide protection to employees which exceed requirements of the federal laws.*

In the safety and health area, for example, many states regulate specifically how old an adolescent must be before employment begins and the age level that must be attained before a young person can operate power-driven machinery.

DEALING WITH GOVERNMENT REPRESENTATIVES

Visits by government inspectors, delivery of subpoenas, and search warrants are a fact of life on the business scene today. Even a small organization should have a policy on what to do when a government inspector or a public official arrives on site.

The intent of the policy should be to leave a positive impression with the government representative and assure management that the matter is being handled well by the personnel office. In some cases the employer may have a legal obligation to provide information to the official or allow admittance to the facility. An OSHA compliance officer, for example, has the right of entry to a workplace, without advance notice, during regular business hours. Management may refuse that entry but OSHA will be quick to obtain a warrant for entry through a court.

Here are suggestions for how to handle visits by government officials and law enforcement officers in a professional manner:

▶ Ensure that the person says who he or she is. A person in uniform is usually well identified with a name and badge. For others ask for a business card or an identification card with photograph.

▶ Determine the purpose of the visit. Most representatives will explain to a manager the reason for the visit; if not, be sure to ask.

► Use a private office or conference room to assure confidentiality. Listen a lot—avoid volunteering information.

► Handle any telephone requests for information cautiously. It may not be a bona fide government representative or police official on the other end of the line. Listen to the request, write down the person's name, title, agency name, telephone number, and address and then return the call to confirm that it is a legitimate government representative.

Your Turn   ► How prepared are you for an OSHA inspection?

UNEMPLOYMENT COMPENSATION

Unemployment compensation (UC) coverages are at the state level, and this seemingly routine process of confirming the termination of an employee can turn out to be an effective cost control mechanism.

Basics of the unemployment compensation system and the distinctions on how unemployment benefit eligibility is established should be mastered in each personnel office. One person in the personnel department should be trained in the handling of UC claims and details of state law on the subject. Each claim should be verified—correct name, social security number, date of layoff or termination, and the reason for termination. In some states a person who is discharged for cause, or quits without good cause, is ineligible for benefits for a specified period of time. Respond to the state's report promptly within the specified time period (otherwise, in some states, the claim is automatically granted) and be prepared to present documentation and support for the company's position.

The unemployment compensation system is designed to pay benefits for persons out of work as defined in state laws and regulations. It is the employer's responsibility to show why a claimant should not receive benefits.

WORKERS' COMPENSATION

Workers' compensation coverages for most employers are at the state level. The basic benefits that are common to all workers' compensation systems are medical treatment, disability pay, and compensation for the permanent effect of an injury or occupational illness.

The basic principle of workers' compensation coverage provides that in exchange for payment of medical costs and disability reimbursement for injuries or job illnesses, the injured employee will not file suit against the employer.

In recent years this no-fault approach has been encroached upon as a number of suits have been filed, over and above workers' compensation coverage, claiming negligence on the part of the employer. In a tort suit, the claimants allege, for example, that the employer's machinery was defective or improperly maintained or the original manufacturer of the machinery supplied defective machinery to the employer. Although small in number these tort suits are increasing and some employee claims for serious injuries are being upheld by the courts.

Employers' Views of Workers' Compensation

The vast majority of employers want injured or occupationally ill employees to receive their proper entitlements under the system of the particular state in which the injury occurred. These positive-thinking employers want the employee to receive quality medical treatment and rehabilitation, and the vast majority will make real efforts to return the injured employee to a job with the company.

From a workers' comp carrier point of view, 85 percent of the cases are straightforward payments of medical and disability benefits for legitimate injuries or job-oriented illnesses. Payment for these claims is processed promptly; the medical provider receives payment and the employee receives disability benefits and is back to the job soon without long-term impairment.

The remaining 15 percent of the claims takes about 90 percent of the effort of employers, insurance carriers, and medical specialists. These are the back injury cases, the repetitive motion injury claims, the potentially fraudulent claims and excessive time away from work, occupational illness claims such as respiratory disorders, hearing loss attributed to noise from the job, stress claims, and the like.

Job injuries are usually incidents of trauma. Occupational illness stemming from the job is frequently less precise and often vague in its relationship to work. While only five percent of the total of all injuries and illnesses are occupational illnesses such as dermatitis, lung disorders, and repetitive motion injuries, these have long-term implications that can result in high workers' comp costs unless detected early and treated promptly.

Employer Actions

What can an employer do to bring about better control of these loss areas?

First, review workers' compensation summary of losses. Workers' compensation carriers and claims-paying agents regularly provide employers with printouts of workers' compensation cases they are handling for the employer. Some carriers produce these reports monthly, others on a quarterly basis, but all typically provide an annual summary of losses with details of each case.

Too often these reports are received, scanned, and promptly go into a file. That is a mistake because at times wrong names and wrong companies are entered into these reports in error and the employer ends up paying compensation for another employer's injured worker. Other mistakes can creep into these computerized reports—wrong diagnoses, overpayments to employees, double payments in error to medical providers, and the like. A careful review of worker's compensation "loss runs" can pay off for the employer.

Another workers' compensation cost area—the setting up of reserves for injury cases—needs particular attention. Carriers typically set up case reserves, which are estimates of future or continuing liability for a case. For example, an employee with an injured foot may have had surgery, hospital, and medical expenses up to a given date. These are known expenses but the employee will require further treatment and possibly rehabilitation through physical and occupational therapy. The estimated costs of future treatment are typically reserved, providing the employer at any time an estimate of the total cost of the case. Quarterly reviews of the status of the reserves are advised because the changing nature of injury cases may make a reserve too low or too high. Employers should demand that the insurance company provide a rationale for highly reserved claims.

Help from the Insurance Carrier

Most workers' compensation carriers want to provide pro-active assistance to the employer in dubious cases or those with potential for malingering or fraud. Good communication between the carrier and the employer's representative is critical to managing this small number of claims.

Remember that carriers receive hundreds of worker's compensation claims each day. So that claims requiring special attention will stand out in the daily work flow at the carrier, the following steps are recommended:

▶ Prompt investigation of the accident (within minutes after the injured employee has received medical treatment and no later than 24 hours).

▶ Know your state's workers' compensation rules, particularly the cause and effect relationship which says that there must be an incident that triggered the injury or a cumulation of exposure that developed into the occupational illness. In the case of a small employer one person should be assigned to monitor compensation claims.

▶ If the employer feels the workers' compensation claim is questionable or if malingering is suspected, the carrier should be asked to conduct a nonmedical lay investigation, including surveillance of the employee's day-to-day activities if necessary. If there is an adequate base of concern, the carrier can arrange for surveillance, but be careful not to entrap or harass the employee.

▶ In many states employees are allowed an initial choice of doctor. In nonroutine or questionable cases most states allow the employer to request an Independent Medical Examination (IME) by a physician or medical specialist of the employer's choice. Results of this examination would be assessed by the carrier along with the comments from the employee's physician to determine the true nature or extent of the injury.

▶ Bill auditing and peer review of medical treatment may be called for so that the employer is reassured that the worker is receiving value for the workers' compensation dollars spent on care for the injured employee.

▶ Be prepared to attend any workers' compensation hearing that may be scheduled on a disputed claim. A "no show" by management representatives usually means concurrence that handling of the claim is acceptable, and the claimant's request may be granted on the spot.

Remember that the carrier is working for you, the employer, and should be communicating well and explaining options to you.

Occupational Disease Claims

Occupational disease claims require special handling and attention. Diseases are normally caused by many factors and work-related exposures may or may not be one of those factors.

For example, loss of a person's hearing can be caused by a number of factors both on-the-job and nonoccupationally related. Continued exposure to high levels of noise at work without the use of hearing protection will result in a decline in hearing. Hearing loss can also come from heredity causes, trauma to the head, diseases and infections, aging, and noisy hobbies and leisure activities. Occupational hearing loss can be effectively prevented by the use of quality hearing protection, properly inserted in the ear canal, and worn at all times in high-noise exposure areas.

While occupational disease claims must be accepted from the employee for processing, accepting company liability should not be inferred or agreed to until an in-depth investigation, medical evaluation, and medical prognosis have been completed.

Modified Duty Programs

A significant control mechanism that can be introduced to control workers' compensation costs is the provision of alternate duty, light work, or restricted duty programs with an employer. Such programs usually provide that employees injured on a job who are capable of doing some work at the facility will be offered easier work, with the approval of the physician, until the employee is able to resume his or her normal duties.

Employees who have suffered more serious injuries are frequently returned to work earlier into easier jobs under such programs until the employee is ready to resume a previous job.

Time off work is not a reward for being injured. A forward-thinking management group can readily find productive and service work to keep such injured persons gainfully employed.

An Employer Who Cares

One of the most significant early steps that an employer can take is to show care and concern for the injured employee. Well-established first aid and medical facilities, staffed with trained medical or first aid personnel, provides a basis of caring.

After an injury an employer's representative who accompanies the injured worker for treatment demonstrates the employer's interest in the welfare of the worker and discourages exaggerated or contrived injuries. Such a step provides the employer valuable early information about the nature and extent of the injury and an opportunity to begin a relationship with the treating physician.

Continued contact and supportive encouragement to the injured worker is also important. Prompt processing of workers' compensation claims forms, contact and assistance to the injured employee's family, and other courtesies will enhance the relationship between management and the injured employee, as well as project a positive employer image to the workforce.

As the employee recovers, ongoing contact, at least weekly, by management representatives will do a lot to keep the employee in a positive attitude, anxious to return to work as soon as physically able.

ASK YOURSELF

► Which information posters are required to be posted at your place of work?

► What is the danger of using "permanent" in describing an employment situation?

► How can you best control workers' compensation costs?

► What current employment-related laws do you feel are unnecessary or redundant?

► What three employment-related laws stand out to you as the most important?

CHAPTER SIX

MANAGING COMPENSATION AND BENEFITS

WAGES AND BENEFITS

An early decision for a manager starting up a business is: "What rates of pay will I offer my employees?" and "What medical and insurance benefits should I provide?"

Wage and benefit levels at start-up companies are often dictated by the wages and salaries that management must pay to attract key employees needed to get the new business underway. But, over time, the purpose of a compensation system should be to attract, retain, and motivate a broad spectrum of high-quality employees at all levels.

As the organization settles down some very basic questions need to be answered. It is often the personnel manager who researches compensation levels and appropriate employee benefits in the community and industry and makes recommendations for a wage and benefit structure to line management. This chapter deals with considerations the personnel manager will face in developing a wage and salary compensation structure for the small business and an employee benefits package such as life insurance, medical coverages, and the like.

Among the considerations will be:

► What are competitive rates of pay for executive, managerial, technical, office, and factory jobs in the area?

► What are the rates for these same jobs in the industry in which the company competes?

► Should the business consider incentive pay, individual piece work, or group bonus arrangements in addition to a base salary?

► What are appropriate benefits in the way of life insurance, medical and hospital, and other benefits for employees in this area and in this industry?

► What can the small business afford?

Other important considerations will include economic trends in the region or nation and the supply and demand trends for critical skills. The personnel manager will also need to investigate other aspects of a compensation package such as pay for working overtime, differentials for afternoon or evening shifts, special pay for persons who are job instructors or group leaders, and geographic differentials for working in high-cost areas of the country.

Discussions should also be held on the need for special pay programs for executives (base pay, annual bonus, long-term incentive pay, special benefits, and perquisites) and for direct sales personnel (salary, commission, or bonus, or all three). Other compensation considerations include cash awards and company stock incentives.

WAGE RATES AND RANGES

Once an employer determines whether it wants to be area-competitive or industry-competitive—or both—some research work is required. Salaries for executives, managers, and some professionals are often determined on a national or regional level; rates of pay for clerical staff and factory workers are usually tied to a geographical area or to community wage relationships.

Obtaining this information may be as simple as visiting local companies and offering to exchange rates of pay for certain key or benchmark classifications of work. Not every company will agree to exchange such information but a cooperative spirit in a local personnel association or chamber of commerce may result in getting this background information.

Frequently, chambers of commerce, state business and industry associations, and consulting firms conduct annual surveys of salaries or wages paid for many common benchmark jobs. This information can be used as a base to set salaries and adjust wages each year based on cost-of-living structure and/or the availability of merit increase funds. Regular information on wage and salary trends is also provided by national organizations such as the American Compensation Association which can be particularly helpful in developing merit increase budgets or pool dollars for merit increase purposes.

Internal/External Relationships

Personnel managers recommending ranges of pay for jobs need to be acutely aware of the importance of maintaining a relationship or spread between jobs of increasing levels of importance and skill and contribution to the business. Supervisors' salary ranges should be higher than the range of the highest-level person supervised. Mechanics should be paid more than operators, and operators paid more than laborers or entry help.

Some companies have found it necessary to deviate from these principles in the case of specialized technical and scientific staff. In some organizations a separate technical salary scale has been developed so that senior scientists, technical consultants, and experienced engineers with specialized expertise are paid in salary ranges comparable to the salary ranges of technical management.

Similarly, professions which are in high demand for personnel—data processing, physical therapy, nursing, for example—may call for ranges to parallel the external marketplace rather than an internal structure.

Other organizations, anxious to increase motivation among workers, may use a "skill based pay" approach, which rewards the employee based on additional knowledge and skills acquired. This approach is used frequently with mechanics to promote greater learning and expertise and gives supervisors greater flexibility in planning work assignments. As an example, in the metal fabricating industry most journeyman mechanics may be paid at job grade 16 but, as they show ability or complete training in additional skills, they are advanced one job grade at a time for being competent in, say, the additional duties of a millwright, machinist, or electrician.

JOB DESCRIPTIONS

Many organizations have found it helpful to develop job descriptions or summaries of job duties to assist in determining wage levels. Written job descriptions outline job responsibilities and duties with factors such as training and experience required for the job, responsibility for operations, mental and physical skill required, and working conditions.

The job description for an experienced secretary, for example, should indicate duties and responsibilities that are more critical than those for a typist. Similarly, a scientist would have one level of responsibility, a senior scientist should have more experience and broader responsibilities, and the manager of a group of scientists would have broad technical experience and responsibilities for managing and directing a staff.

Job descriptions are the starting point to developing a wage structure which determines the relative worth of each job to the organization so that grades or levels of responsibility can be assigned to each job.

A good set of job descriptions will also assist employment staff in their recruiting and selection activities, and medical and safety staff in the correct placement of employees consistent with their physical abilities.

Although no government law at this time requires an employer to develop job descriptions, the Americans with Disabilities Act references the subject. The ADA says that persons with disabilities may be required to perform the essential functions of a job, with or without some type of reasonable accommodation, but such a person could not be required to perform the lesser or marginal functions of the job as a basis for disqualification in the selection process.

FRINGE BENEFITS

"How many holidays shall we give our employees?" "What sort of vacation plan do we need to provide?" These are questions often facing a personnel manager in a start-up situation or when improvements to fringe benefits are being considered.

Again, patterns of practice in the community, region or state will often be a factor determining these benefit levels. In some cases a major union agreement in a community will influence the predominant levels of fringe benefits.

Local chambers of commerce, state business and industry associations, and professional and trade associations often develop surveys of these fringe benefit levels or maintain data banks with this information, which the personnel professional can access through membership.

And a word of caution is needed here to managers of small businesses. The company may provide a number of weeks of vacation for its employees but key players in a small business, preoccupied with the success of the enterprise, may say that vacations are for someone else. If they take any time off it tends to be a long weekend or an extended business trip with a few days of R and R. But it should be more than that.

Busy business managers need to break away—to take time away to rest their minds from the daily grind. Personnel administrators in fledgling businesses need to remind their principals of the value of vacation/rest time to recharge their (human) batteries.

MERIT RATINGS AND PERFORMANCE APPRAISALS

How will the employer pay for good performance? Will a merit increase program apply or will employees automatically receive step increases based on longevity in the job? Should annual lump sum payments be considered in lieu of so-called merit increases? Or will the employer increase wages by applying cost-of-living adjustments? Or should an incentive plan be considered? Or will some version of each of these be considered?

These are questions that the personnel manager needs to research and then develop recommendations so that good work by employees is rewarded and motivation remains high.

First, let's discuss merit increases. The amount of a merit increase associated with a given level of performance varies depending on inflation levels, labor market increases to wages, and company performance, among other factors. As the name implies the amount of a merit increase should be tied to meritorious performance—the top performers being awarded higher amounts.

Performance of organizational units can also be paid for through profit sharing and similar variable pay plans. When teams are managed as intact business units, team bonuses can be paid for performance.

Anniversary or Focus Dates

Another question often arises about the task that many line managers view as laborious, the job of completing appraisals: Should employees receive performance reviews on their anniversary date (of hire or promotion) or should all employees be reviewed in a given time period, say January each year? Each approach has advantages and disadvantages.

Pay reviews tied in with an employee's anniversary date provide greater consideration to the individual employee and allow more time for the supervisor to prepare the appraisal before meeting with the individual employee.

Using a focus date approach allows managers to evaluate all eligible employees in comparison to one another in a single time period, providing more concentrated reviews and better comparisons of performance.

On the negative side, a set date each year requires a bulge of work for managers. Focus review dates can also cause organizational tension because the month of review can prompt rumors, heightened expectations, and may take on an unnecessary urgency as rushed supervisors try to satisfy the entire staff.

Training Supervisors to Complete Performance Evaluations

In many companies performance evaluations are tied in with merit increases. To accomplish that approach effectively, supervisors must be trained in performance management and how to complete the performance appraisal form objectively and fairly. The system must gain credibility with employees by rewarding higher levels of performance with higher levels of merit increases.

Performance appraisals need to be completed fairly but accurately. An honest critique of an employee's work is essential if the employee is to have fair warning of the need for improvement. Good performance should be confirmed formally through the evaluation process.

Confidentiality in the Personnel Department

Personnel offices handle and process much confidential information and one of the most sensitive areas—wages and salaries—requires special measures to protect confidentiality of the information. This is a requirement in most companies, although some organizations widely publish the salary ranges for jobs and the earnings level of incumbents. Earnings of top officers in publicly owned companies are printed in the corporate annual report of the organization.

Personnel representatives should discuss salary information *only* with those with a need to know—usually the immediate supervisor or manager of the employee involved. Salary and appraisal information should be kept in individual file folders in locked files. Computerized salary information should be safeguarded.

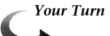

Your Turn

▶ Where do I currently store salary and appraisal information?

REQUIRED AND OPTIONAL BENEFITS

There are a number of legally required programs, many of which are at a cost to the employer and benefit the employee—social security, survivor benefits and disability insurance. Employees also contribute to the cost of some of these programs.

But many employers go beyond these federal and state mandates to provide additional benefits such as medical insurance plans, pensions, sick leave payments, long- and short-term disability payments, life insurance coverage, dental and vision plans, and tuition reimbursement programs.

Benefit Plans and Pensions

Federal laws at this time do not require employers to provide medical and disability benefits to employees, although many employers do so. A few states require employer-funded short-term disability plans.

The purpose of any disability benefit plan is to partially replace income lost because of disability. Short-term disability plans generally provide benefits for up to 26 weeks in the expectation that the employee will return to work. A few states require that any short-term disability benefits for workers be arranged through a state disability benefits payment plan, although employers may choose to provide coverage in excess of the basic state plan.

Some companies also offer long-term disability benefits (LTD) to partially replace income of persons so severely ill or disabled that they are unable to be gainfully employed or unable to return to work. Long-term disability benefits often begin after 26 weeks of disability and the person on disability may also be eligible for Social Security (disability benefits) or other mandated benefit programs.

Similarly, no federal law at this time requires private employers to provide a pension plan or retirement coverage for employees but many employers choose to do so or offer a 401-K plan where an employer matches all or part of an employee contribution to a tax-deferred savings plan. Employer-sponsored pension plans have been scaled back in recent years and private pensions now provide only about 20 percent of retirement income for workers. As a result the 401-K plans have received increasing attention from employers and high interest by employees in the past decade.

The whole area of benefit planning and administration is complex and intertwined with requirements of government laws. Any business with a group insurance, pension, or 401-K plan will do well to draw on professional benefit planning expertise for guidance in establishing and maintaining the plans.

In 1974 the federal government enacted ERISA (Employee's Retirement Income Security Act) to protect the pensions of workers enrolled in employer-sponsored pension plans. ERISA requires pension plan sponsors to set aside money annually to pay for current and future benefits. Pension benefits for widowed and divorced spouses have been added and disclosure requirements were implemented to keep workers and retirees informed about their benefit entitlements. More than 41 million workers in this country are now protected by ERISA's provisions.

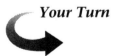

Your Turn

► Now that you are in business interviewing people for jobs with your company, what do you think these people are prioritizing in their job search in terms of salary and/or benefits?

COBRA COVERAGE

The federal COBRA (Comprehensive Budget Reconciliation Act) requires employers offering medical insurance to allow terminated workers to continue coverage at a small premium over the employer's cost for certain periods of time following termination. Employees must pay the premiums directly to the insurance carrier. The law applies to employers with 20 or more employees in the previous year.

The entitlement to benefits under COBRA is triggered by certain qualifying events and may apply to an employee, an employee's spouse, and employee's dependent children. The entitlement to benefits lasts either 18 or 36 months depending on the qualifying event, unless the employee was terminated for "gross misconduct." Some states have coverages which extend longer than the federal coverage period.

Beneficiaries have the right to elect coverage identical to their coverage previously provided under the plan. Personnel managers need to be aware of federal provisions and any state coverages which exceed the federal benefit levels.

The employer must notify employees and their spouses in writing of their rights under COBRA.

EMPLOYEE ASSISTANCE PROGRAMS

Alcoholism and drug abuse are treatable illnesses and many employers originally established employee assistance programs (EAPs) to deal with these concerns. But EAPs are also designed to assist employees with problems that affect job performance, family problems, stress, elder care, and financial and legal concerns. Programs vary widely in the services offered.

For the small business the most practical and cost-effective approach to an employee assistance program is to tie in with an EAP organization serving the community so that employees can contact the agency directly with the employer not even being aware that the contact has been made.

In most instances potential users of EAP services call a toll-free number, briefly disclosing their problem and are then referred to a counselor with expertise in the area of need. EAPs focus on identifying current problems and providing coping skills.

Whatever type of service is provided employers should publicize availability of EAPs to their workers, emphasizing that contact is confidential. Fees to the employer are usually based on a per-head charge for the total number of employees in the workforce, rather than on the cost of individual referrals, which protects confidentiality.

ASK YOURSELF

► What are the benefits of having written job descriptions for positions in your company?

► Who is entitled to COBRA benefits?

► As an employer, are you required to provide medical and dental insurance plans?

► If your were crafting an ideal package of benefits for a salaried professional, what would you include? Why?

CHAPTER
SEVEN

EMPLOYEE
RELATIONS
ACTIVITIES

CHAPTER SEVEN

EMPLOYEE RELATIONS

Once a business is up and operational many of the day-to-day dealings between management and employees are characterized as "employee relations." If some or all of the employees are unionized, the relationships may be called "labor relations."

Business executives look to human resource managers to guide them in their day-to-day dealings with workers. The approach can be friendly, cooperative, stiff, adversarial, autocratic, or bureaucratic—depending on the leadership of the management group.

Most large organizations develop personnel policy manuals as a guide to managers in dealings with employees. Even small businesses should seriously consider this even if, at the start, it is as basic as accumulating policy letters and memos on employee relations matters.

This chapter covers a number of issues the small business owner or manager should consider in developing a desirable work atmosphere.

In recent years the most successful employee relations approaches allow maximum freedom of expression and involvement of employees. In these approaches, worker committees and employee involvement programs replace traditional forms of supervision.

EMPLOYEE COMPLAINTS

Employees are better informed about their rights these days and less willing to trust an employer than in years past. Part of the task of creating a positive employee relations atmosphere is dealing with employee complaints, investigating those matters and trying to solve legitimate employee concerns.

A clear determination needs to be made at the start—should employee concerns be handled in the personnel department or referred back to the line manager for investigation and handling? Even in a small business, a clear policy from the management level is critical. In some organizations the supervisor may seek guidance and help from the personnel department but the line manager is charged with the responsibility of investigating and handling the matter.

If some or all of the complaints are to be handled in the personnel department, then these professionals need to be good listeners, dig to get at the facts, and then try to resolve the complaint within the framework of company policies and existing law.

Employee concerns about discrimination and sexual harassment require a well-publicized company procedure that promptly brings these concerns to senior management attention for investigation.

PROMOTIONS AND TRANSFERS

One of the questions concerning a job opening—even in a young company—will likely be: "Do we have anyone inside who can fill this vacancy?" Formal policies on promotions and transfers will be an early item on a personnel manager's agenda.

In filling promotions from within, consideration should be given to:

- Employee's record of satisfactory work

- Length of service with the organization

- Previous training for the area of interest

- Attendance record

- Recent performance evaluations

- Employee interest in the new position

- Any testing that may be required for the person to qualify for the new work

In some professional and technical disciplines a license of professional or trade status may be required.

The personnel manager can assist the organization greatly by helping to draft policies on transfer and promotion so that internal applicants with matching qualifications are given leading consideration for vacancies.

In small organizations these policies may be unofficial, but as the organization grows a written policy and procedure will make for consistency and fair treatment.

Job Postings

Job posting is often thought of as an employee relations activity used only in large organizations. Certainly, in a small business everybody knows everybody else and there may not be the need for a formal process to bring openings to the attention of employees—and employee interests and qualifications to the attention of management.

However, a job posting system that announces openings in a formal way (through a bulletin board, for instance) tends to minimize favoritism and reduces employee dissatisfaction. A short posting time (typically three work days) will allow supervisors time to evaluate candidates, yet fill the job promptly and get on with production. Employees on vacation or leave can be protected by allowing them to preregister for openings of interest that may occur when they are away.

Companies with experience with a successful job posting activity do not post every job. Many companies post only jobs above entry-level and do not publicize temporary openings or jobs involving lateral transfers.

Promotions from Within . . . But

Many companies believe that they can be successful in the long term by promoting from within wherever possible. Such a policy enhances loyalty, long-term tenure with the company, and a workforce that is broadly trained in many aspects of the business. Many small companies develop their strength and growth in exactly that way.

But there are some negatives to a universal emphasis on promotion from within. That approach can result in inbreeding, the narrowing of the perspective of key managers and workers. It can result in staleness, lethargy, and even a business decline.

That is the reason some companies prefer to hire some key jobs from outside the organization—even outside the particular industry. New technical, professional or managerial talent can gently raise questions about present practices and bring fresh perspective to managers.

DISCIPLINE AND TERMINATION

Good employees will want to perform at or above standards of productivity, quality, and service. But in every organization, large or small, there is a small percentage of employees who do not perform up to expectations. This must be dealt with so that the work of good performers is not dragged down and morale and efficiency lowered.

Many businesses subscribe to the principle of "progressive discipline" unless the facts of the case warrant immediate suspension or termination. In most organizations progressive means counseling or warning to the employee on the first offense. Repeat offenses are followed by written warnings, disciplinary suspension, and finally, termination. The range of penalties before termination depends on the organization's view of the disciplinary process and the particular incident at hand.

After company policies are established and communicated to employees, managers and supervisors must be trained on how to administer the policies in an even-handed manner.

It's also a good practice to have the personnel professional review terminations *before* the action takes place. An employee who feels discharged wrongfully may file a lawsuit against the organization and/or resort to discrimination charges if he or she is a member of a protected class.

A discipline process should include the considerations of promptness, privacy, and positivity.

Promptness

The infraction should be dealt with promptly—immediately after the incident or, if time is needed to investigate, within 24 hours of the incident. Lateness in responding can be interpreted as approval of the action.

If the incident is serious it may be appropriate to place the employee on suspension, pending results of an investigation.

Privacy

The investigation should be conducted in a private office or meeting room. The employee should not be embarrassed in front of others.

Positivity

A constructive and positive tone should be established for the disciplinary hearing. Be specific on the infraction. Ask for the employee's side of the incident. Ask for the employee's suggestions on how to improve. Avoid comparing one employee to others. Explain what the action means to the company and to the individual.

Accentuate the positives wherever possible. Emphasize the positive results that a change in behavior can bring. Suggest a follow-up session in a week's time to discuss the suggestions developed in the meeting.

Note: Don't wait until the annual performance appraisal to deliver criticism! By the time the annual review comes around there should be no surprises.

The manner in which an employee is terminated often has a great deal of bearing on whether the employee files a charge or lawsuit against the organization. The personnel officer should review the situation, ideally in advance, and be satisfied that:

▶ The termination follows company procedures on discipline or termination

▶ Abides by federal and state legislation

- ▶ Meets company's financial procedural requirements in terms of final wage payments, vacation pay, and coverage under laws such as COBRA (federal) and any state extensions of that coverage

- ▶ In the case of involuntary terminations, if company policies so provide, outplacement counseling or transitional job finding assistance to the person

Conducting an Investigation

Personnel administrators and line managers are trying to find out "What happened?" as they investigate a workplace incident. But how that investigation is conducted is critical to balancing fair treatment and discipline to the offender while protecting the company in the event of a discrimination claim.

Although most laws do not require a formal investigation, the courts tend to look to the fairness and adequacy of an investigation, and may well penalize a company that has not performed an investigation of a discrimination complaint. In the sexual harassment area, an employer who knows of—or should know of—such harassment and does not thoroughly investigate faces the potential for substantial liability.

With discrimination claims, an employer who does not promptly and properly investigate such complaints can be subject to punitive damages. The employer faces liability not only for economic damages, but for emotional distress, pain, suffering and humiliation, and other damages. Federal discrimination laws also allow for payment of the successful employee's legal fees.

Here is how to proceed. (Remember to keep an open mind until the matter has been thoroughly investigated.)

1. Interview and obtain a written statement from the complainant. This should help pin down exactly what the concern is and helps eliminate frivolous complaints. A complainant will often be reluctant to put such statements in writing. In serious circumstances, it may be appropriate to take the statement under oath.

2. Get the names of any potential witnesses from the complainant, interview all witnesses, and either obtain statements from them or keep detailed notes on the information provided.

3. Interview the employee who is alleged to be the offending party and obtain a written statement from that person. Under some circumstances having this statement made under oath may be appropriate.

4. The decision (including any corrective or disciplinary action to be taken) should be given to the complainant and the alleged offender.

Assure the complaining party and all witnesses that any retaliation for their actions or statements is illegal and will not be tolerated by the company.

In some sensitive investigations, it may be important to have another person, preferably another manager, involved in the investigation or as a witness during the interview process.

It may be difficult to do, but managers should be careful not to be influenced by the fact that one employee is more valuable to the company than the other when making the determination.

In sensitive investigations (involving theft, for example) HR managers should consult with in-house counsel or an experienced outside employment attorney before starting an investigation. If the investigation is conducted at the direction of an attorney, the information may be considered privileged and confidential in the event of a lawsuit.

In the case of employee theft or criminal misconduct, the employer may decide to pursue the matter in civil or criminal courts. However, extreme caution should be exercised in conducting such investigations or in starting legal action, since overzealous or unfounded charges may subject the employer to liability for malicious prosecution, defamation, and invasion of privacy.

A short cooling off period while investigating a serious complaint may be necessary. A suspension from work with or without pay may be appropriate, but if such action is taken personnel managers should conduct an investigation promptly so that the period of uncertainty does not last too long.

Your Turn

► Do you feel you have the skills needed to conduct an investigation of a complaint?

The Supervisor's Role in Discipline

A key role of a supervisor is a willingness and ability to confront employees with performance problems and take appropriate corrective action. Careful, documented action is more likely to improve the employee's work performance and decrease the employer's exposure to employment discrimination and wrongful discharge claims.

Supervisors may need assistance from the personnel professional in investigating facts surrounding employee misconduct, illegal activity in the workplace, or behavior that is detrimental to efficiency at the job site. But it is the supervisor's responsibility—*not* that of the personnel professional—to extend and apply discipline.

Disciplinary matters involving employees require due process—a protection of the United States Constitution. The complaining employee should be heard and the accused should be asked to give their side of the story. The supervisor and the personnel representative must be open minded until all facts are in. In serious cases it may be wise to consult with the company's attorney.

The investigation should be handled in a confidential manner with disclosure only to those persons who have a need to know. All parties involved should be reminded of the need to maintain confidentiality.

The final disciplinary action should be appropriate to the seriousness of the complaint, and both the complainant and accused should be advised.

ATTENDANCE AND LATENESS

Employers can reasonably expect employees to come to work regularly and to report to work on time. Absence and lateness are a problem that confronts line managers and many personnel professionals early in their job.

Companies recognize that some employee absences will occur, and they allow for a number of paid sick days or personal days during the course of a year. Other companies take a stricter view of the problem—employees are expected to be in regular attendance and at work on time. These organizations have set up no-fault absentee policies or "leave banks" that allow employees a prescribed number of days absent each year for any reason—valid or otherwise. After that predetermined number of days, discipline occurs quickly and termination may follow.

Many organizations have found it necessary to establish absence-control programs to remedy the problem and, failing that, to discipline or dismiss offenders.

A key ingredient of an attendance and lateness control policy is documentation; that is, a list is kept for each employee of absences or lateness and the stated reasons for those absences. This is then compared to other workers or the average incidence for the facility. Personnel departments are often asked to record the documentation of absences and the reason for the absences.

EMPLOYEE PRIVACY

Workplace privacy issues have taken on new meaning these days. Personnel managers need to be aware of federal and state laws that apply to the collection of information on employees and the dissemination of information internally or to designated outsiders. In some cases it will be a wise protection for the employer to ask the employee's permission in writing to give the information to outsiders.

Even small business managers need to be sensitive to the area of employee privacy. A key maxim should be: Make sure the information is job related and the person requesting the information has a need to know. You might also request the employee's written permission to release the information.

DISCRIMINATION CLAIMS

A person in a protected class may allege discrimination and unlawful employment practices by the employer. Under federal law a protected-class person is one who may face job discrimination because of their sex, age (40 and over), race, national origin, religion, disability or handicap, or being a disabled veteran or veteran of the Vietnam war. Many state and local laws expand this definition to include sexual orientation.

The enforcing agencies for such laws are the Equal Employment Opportunity Commission at the federal level and fair employment practice (FEP) agencies at the state level. The employee files the charge in writing, and the employer is notified. The employer has an opportunity to provide defenses for the company action and prove a business necessity for its conduct.

LABOR ORGANIZATIONS

Under the National Labor Relations Act of 1935 (also known as the Wagner Act) employees were granted broad rights to organize into labor unions and to bargain collectively with the employer. The act protects the rights of employees who choose to organize, join, or assist labor organizations or to engage in "concerted activities" such as strikes, boycotts, and picketing. The act also prohibits employer conduct identified as "unfair labor practices" that would interfere with rights, such as discouraging union membership or refusing to bargain in good faith.

The act also established an administrative agency, the National Labor Relations Board (NLRB), to conduct elections by secret ballot to determine union certification and to remedy unfair labor practices.

A union will typically propose in its request for certification the composition of the bargaining unit—usually a broad perspective of employees that the union would hope to include. Under the law management may propose that certain classifications be excluded—for example, the exclusion from a potential bargaining unit of persons who are managers and supervisors, professional employees, plant guards, and confidential employees.

Nonunion Establishments

Employees tend to join unions if they feel the need to protect themselves against arbitrary and unreasonable acts of management.

The reason unions form in many organizations is often poor first-line supervision or disinterested higher levels of management.

Employees tend to avoid union membership when they identify with company management and view union membership as adversarial or unnecessary. These employees are generally satisfied when wages and benefits are competitive in the community or with what the union has negotiated by the union in other workplaces.

Early in the game a business manager needs to determine whether to provide employees maximum opportunity for expression, thus hoping that the small company atmosphere may make the need for unionization unnecessary.

To increase the opportunity for a union-free environment, business managers should consider the following:

▶ Establish a written company policy including the company's goals and individual performance standards. Communicate the policies through meetings and an employee handbook.

▶ Clarify compensation practices and benefits provisions. Pledge regular reviews, usually annually, of wages and benefits and other conditions of employment.

▶ Investigate and handle employee complaints promptly informally or through a formal complaint process.

▶ Let employees know where they stand. Appraise employee performance regularly and provide training of managers and supervisors to do this effectively.

Your Turn   ***Think about:***

▶ If you could shape an ideal way to deal with employees reporting to you, what would you include in the approach?

SEVERANCE PAY

Most small businesses are more interested in adding new employees and growing their business rather than who terminates voluntarily or is released from employment.

Most states do not have any requirement to provide company pay to a person who leaves employment voluntarily other than for any unused vacation time. While most such employees provide notice of intent to terminate, some employers choose to have the employee leave promptly and pay the person in lieu of notice.

But what about the employee who is terminated involuntarily due to downsizing or the elimination of a position? Employers—even small organizations—need to consider this area of personnel policy. A 1995 survey by the Society for Human Resource Management showed that 83 percent of the 250 organizations who responded to the survey indicated that terminated employees were entitled to some form of severance pay. About half of the respondents said their severance package provided one week of pay for each year of service, and roughly one-quarter of the respondents said their severance package provided two weeks of pay for each year of service.

Surprisingly, nearly 23 percent of respondents said employees are eligible for severance pay even when termination is based on poor performance.

SAFETY AND OCCUPATIONAL HEALTH

Accidents can and do occur on the job and risks of varying degrees of seriousness exist in every manufacturing plant, distribution center, and office in the country. The small business is a natural setting for an effective safety and health program as workers know one another well and there is strong motivation to work safely.

The traditional safety committee with representation from each department is a workable activity for the small business. With management support these committees can bring hazards and unsafe work practices to management attention and get them corrected. Those steps also helps lower workers' compensation costs.

There are many approaches to safety and occupational health that work—as evidenced by fewer accidents, lower workers' compensation costs, and higher employee morale and productivity. The most effective activities are those lead by line managers who understand the negative cost implications of accidents and want to preserve the safety and good health of their employees. Personnel professionals can certainly facilitate the safety process but for long-term effectiveness it must be the line managers who are responsible for implementing the program.

A number of approaches to safety and health in a small organization are outlined in Appendix IV.

DRESS CODES

Many business managers have accepted more leisurely work attire for employees by asking themselves, "Is formal business attire *really* required for every position?"

Casual attire helps lower status barriers at a time when many organizations are inviting greater employee involvement in their businesses. It can be looked on as a perk—allowing employees to save money on business attire by buying clothing they can use on both workdays and weekends.

Personnel managers developing a dress code policy should consider what image the business wants to present. That image should revolve around business needs and the image the employer is seeking to present.

Consider also the job that the person holds. Dress codes for a bank's platform officer or a teller who meets the public every day may necessarily be different from staff in the computer room. In a factory the kind of attire appropriate for the front office is not the same as on the production floor where the work environment can involve dust, grease, and other contaminants. Customary and safe work attire for a welder, for example, is a head shield, heavy protective gloves, and an apron.

You can invite employee input to the development of a dress code policy. This will help assure a "pre-sell" of the ultimate policy—which should reflect business necessity, safety considerations, and an effort to accommodate employee desires. Managers need to set the example on the new dress code. In its final form the policy should outline the style of dress, responsibilities of employees in keeping their attire neat, and the possible consequences for violations of the policy.

Human resources managers should oversee that the policy reflects legitimate business necessity, thus avoiding claims of discrimination from limitations on clothing or grooming. Like all other conditions of employment, dress code standards must be nondiscriminatory and must be applied uniformly to all employees regardless of race, color, sex, national origin, or religion.

PREVENTIVE ACTIONS

In any employment relationship some problems will occur. How problems are handled has a major impact on a company's risk of unionization or expensive litigation—as well as general morale and productivity level.

To prevent problems, the human resource specialist can address these issues:

► Has the company developed a published, written policy on major organizational problems, such as on sexual harassment, or notifying employees of lay-offs? If not, is there an informal practice widely known and consistent for all employees?

► Is there an operating *procedure* to support each of these *policies*? For example, how are lay-offs going to be handled? Or what steps are available to an employee complaining of sexual harassment?

► Are the roles of the immediate supervisor versus the human resources specialist spelled out in the policy regarding record-keeping, discipline, and so on. Is there a policy on progressive discipline for most incidents— and is it consistent for all employees?

► Is the employee who is the subject of the complaint a member of a protected class? Protected classes may include anyone who is female, a minority, a veteran, a person age 40 or older, an individual with a disability, or a person whose religion or national origin is protected under federal, state, or local law.

ASK YOURSELF

▶ Who in your organization is responsible for handling employee complaints?

▶ What are the advantages and disadvantages of promoting from within the organization?

▶ What is "progressive discipline"?

▶ Why do you think workers join unions? Why do others shy away from union membership?

CHAPTER EIGHT

COMMUNICATION FACTORS

COMMUNI-CATION ISSUES

Most employees have a natural inquisitiveness about the company they work for. They want to know about business developments within the company, the company's plans for the future, and how they can assist in achieving goals of the business. Communication with workers occurs constantly and its effectiveness can be the cornerstone of business success.

This chapter deals with improving communication from business owners to employees and—the reverse—communication from workers to management. A good way to enhance two-way communication is through employee involvement in work and business activities.

Communication on the job most often involves the immediate supervisor and an employee—the supervisor telling the worker about a change in a production schedule, repairs to a particular machine, quality specifications of a new product, safety priorities in the department, and so on. In turn, the employee communicates up the line to various levels of management that schedules are being met, machinery needs to be purchased or repaired, and similar issues.

Communication in a small business has the potential to be more effective than communication in larger organizations. Word-of-mouth communication is the most effective method of communication. The small business has fewer organizational layers and communication is easier to manage when employees and supervisors are well-known to each other and often work side by side.

As businesses grow and time for communication becomes stretched, additional techniques must be brought into play. To supplement one-on-one communications, small group meetings can be held to cover subjects of general concern. Larger group get-togethers save managers' time; all employees have an opportunity to ask questions and managers are assured that all employees have received the same information.

Supplementary Communications Aids

Facility bulletin boards are often the responsibility of the personnel department. These traditional communication devices can leave a positive impression—or an impression of disorganization. Government-required postings should be clean, up-to-date, and neatly tacked at the four corners of the poster. Government inspectors making an official visit to the facility will often check the bulletin board as a preliminary indication of how important compliance is to the company. If required postings are not there, the company will hear about it or get a citation.

Some companies typically allow a two week posting time for company notices or bulletins. Before the notice is posted a typist inserts a "post" date, and a "remove" date two weeks later allowing these boards to be kept fresh and up-to-date. For permanent notices the words "Permanent - Do Not Remove" are inserted in a lower corner of the notice.

Multimedia

Today there's virtually no limit to the types of media that can be used, even in a small business, to communicate company information to employees and employee questions and concerns up the line to supervisors and management.

Newsletters or company magazines are also used to communicate important information. Suggestion boxes are used in some companies to get employee ideas to management's attention. Electronic mail and electronic bulletin boards are used increasingly in industry. Large in-plant video display screens can also communicate production, quality, and safety messages to workers on the production floor. Larger companies have their own in-company television networks and use videotaped messages from company officials in their communication programs.

Important information such as a new merit increase or salary administration policy requires careful communication. And changes in employee benefits often require a combination of all these communication techniques—a general announcement of benefit changes, employee meetings, perhaps an explanatory brochure, annual statements of benefit coverages, and a revised employee booklet which summarizes all benefit coverages.

Communication is particularly important when negative information has to be communicated to employees—such as downsizing, layoffs, or consolidation of benefit coverages.

Employee Handbooks

An employee handbook is a particularly good way of communicating important information to new hires.

Many progressive employers—even small businesses—have found that an employee handbook is an excellent way to communicate company policies to employees. Employee handbooks in large organizations tend to be printed, but for a small business, a handbook turned out on a word processor will suffice.

Handbooks can also fulfill a company's legal requirements to communicate certain issues in writing, by providing an alternate to letters.

A handbook is usually directed to new employees, telling them basic information about the company, its benefits, and what employees need to know to be successful on the job. Typical handbooks cover employment policies, equal employment opportunity, employment of relatives, job posting, access to personnel files, compensation practices such as work hours, pay practices, overtime pay, performance reviews and the like, time off arrangements such as vacations, holidays and personal leave, highlights of group health and medical benefits, and employee conduct on the job.

Disclaimer language should be displayed prominently in the handbook, saying that the handbook is *not* considered a contract and that the employer and the employee are free to discontinue the employment arrangement at any time for any reason (this is the employment-at-will disclaimer).

The disclaimer should also say that contents of the handbook are subject to modification at the discretion of the company, reserving its right to change policies and employee benefit programs, premiums, and employee contributions or deductibles at any time. In the employee benefits section, mention should be made of the Summary Plan Description Booklets (SPDs) of benefit plans which are separate documents the employee can refer to for details.

Language on termination in the handbook should be very general, with no procedural or other guarantees listed. If a sudden change in business conditions should occur, or if an employee commits some serious offense, management should have the flexibility to deal with the employee or to adjust the size of the workforce.

Management should include its internal complaint procedures in the handbook, encouraging employees to resolve complaints within the company. Particular emphasis should be given to the employer's compliant resolution procedure addressing employee concerns about sexual harassment.

Revising a handbook as necessary is important so that the document is current with company philosophy and policy and changing federal, state, and local laws. Any new version of the handbook should be dated on the front cover as well as dated inside with the additional statement that this edition cancels all previous editions of the handbook.

An experienced human resource professional should review the draft of the handbook. Then legal counsel should review the final version before it goes to the printer.

A carefully prepared and worded handbook can enhance employee relations and help ensure uniform and fair supervisory treatment of employees. A good handbook can help reduce grievances, discrimination charges, and employee lawsuits.

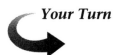

Your Turn ► When was the last time you revised your employee handbook? If you don't have one, why not?

MANAGING THE RUMOR MILL

A good program of communications to employees will do a great deal to quash rumors and bring accurate information to employees and management.

Rumors are born when employees can't get the information they want from their immediate supervisor or from management. In some cases a few disgruntled employees will start rumors as retribution against management.

It's important for the personnel professional to listen to rumors and stay tuned to informal communication channels. Don't try to kill the grapevine—it will always exist. Try to know what's on it and take appropriate communication actions to correct inaccuracies.

Here are some suggestions for managing the rumor mill:

► Share as much information as possible with employees. Information about important company developments should get to employees before it gets to the news media or community.

► The computer has come to the aid of management for fast communication to employees—some CEO's use electronic mail to tell employees of new, important business developments.

► Communicate face to face wherever possible and allow time for employee questions. Have top managers address significant issues as quickly as possible.

► Some large organizations set up a rumor hotline with a toll-free number to call. Give employees access to a key management person to answer their questions as honestly as possible.

WORK RULES

Some companies call them plant rules; others soften the title by labeling them standards of conduct or guidelines for behavior. No matter what the title, these lists of "dos and don'ts on the job are what the employer expects in the way of personal conduct at work and what the penalties will be for misbehavior.

Some companies do not believe in these types of regulations, reasoning that adult workers know what is right and wrong. But in many companies new hires receive a copy of plant rules during orientation, and as changes are made the workforce is asked to acknowledge receiving updated copies.

Work rules typically list an employer's view on items such as the importance of attendance and being at the job on time, restricted areas for eating and smoking, a rule of no soliciting on company property, prohibition of alcohol and drugs on company premises, use of company telephones, and the like.

Plant rules should be reviewed at least annually or when changes in company policy or federal or state laws occur.

These suggestions should be kept in mind when developing plant rules:

- ▶ The tone of work rules should be positive and upbeat, placing responsibility on the individual employee to use common sense and good judgement in conduct at work.

- ▶ Each rule should be reviewed to make sure that it does not violate a federal or state discrimination law. Plant rules must be able to stand up to the scrutiny of government investigators who may be investigating a charge by a present or former employee. These compliance officers will often ask if the employer has company rules, whether they are posted and publicized widely, and how management has applied discipline in similar cases.

► The employer should retain the right to establish reasonable rules controlling employee conduct. Wording about discipline and penalties should be general such as "including, but not limited to, the following . . ." so that management retains broad powers in this area.

► Progressive discipline is generally regarded as positive, but employers should not get trapped into a policy of progressive discipline for every offense. In a serious incident the employer may want to place the employee on suspension while the matter is investigated, or convert the suspension to a termination.

► For a unionized workforce, plant rules are one of the conditions of employment. While plant rule changes should be communicated to the union and their input requested, management should not require the union's approval of the rules nor should management be prepared to negotiate the rules with the union.

A good step to getting greater acceptance of work rules is to provide new hires with a copy and ask for their written acknowledgment that they have received and read a copy.

COMMUNICATING NEGATIVE INFORMATION

Personnel professionals are asked many questions . . . about work practices, benefit coverages—even employees trying to stretch a company policy to their advantage. Sometimes the answer to an employee's request has to be a polite but firm "No."

How that negative decision is communicated can influence

- How the information is accepted

- The employee relations atmosphere in the facility

- Enhanced or lowered reputation of the personnel person who delivers the information

Advising a department about reduced hours of work or lay-offs or telling a plant about reduction in benefit coverages are not easy tasks. How can the communicating of negative news be improved? Here are a few suggestions:

▶ Listen attentively to the request, even if you suspect your answer will be "no." Be courteous and polite; there will be time to deliver the decision.

▶ Speak in words that your audience will understand, translating any unknown jargon to lay terms.

▶ Tell employees the truth. You needn't apologize for saying "no," but you must be sure the employee feels that you have been honest. Be prepared with the specific reasons that the request must be denied.

▶ Speak slowly and watch the person's eyes and facial expressions to see if they are comprehending what you are saying. In some cases a written summary or a letter with reasons for the decision may be helpful to hand to the employee at the end of the meeting.

▶ Time is required for information to settle in. Make yourself available the next day to answer questions the person may have about the decision.

Communicating bad news is not an easy assignment but with care and planning the negative impact can be reduced—and the session may even be turned into a positive employee relations contact.

Your Turn

Speaking of communicating,

▶ How do you like to receive information from your superior?

▶ What poor practices do you see in that person's communication style that you would improve on?

INVOLVING EMPLOYEES

Even before there was talk about employee involvement and team playing, athletic sports activities had shown the value of team members interacting well together to achieve a common goal.

Organizational psychologists speak about the importance of working together, of sharing ideas, and trying to solve problems for the common good of the business. In some companies this pooling of ideas is handled through regular department staff meetings; in other organizations the problem solving approach is handled through a quality improvement team (QIT) or some similar form of activity.

A small business lends itself particularly well to employee involvement because employees are well known to one another and organizational barriers are few.

Success of employee involvement activities will involve merging a number of different personalities into an effective working activity. The person who leads the employee team is usually chosen because of leadership abilities. The emphasis should be on team success, rather than individual recognition. Success revolves around persons willing to subjugate their independence to one of interdependence with other team members.

In typical work team activities, team members examine one or more of the department's activities, trying to determine what works well and what does not. The best teams allow time for ideas to settle in. They try to arrive at decisions by consensus, or at least a majority. Each team member should have a chance to speak their mind, then be willing to support the decision of the majority. That involves a spirit of compromise while the activity is given a fair try-out (with results monitored carefully). There's a great feeling of accomplishment when the team completes an assignment well.

Members of employee involvement teams in a production environment typically have these responsibilities:

▶ Learn and be prepared to perform other jobs on the team

▶ Plan and prioritize daily work schedules with other team members in order to meet quality and customer requirements

▶ Read specification sheets and any other written instructions that help meet production standards

Participation in employee involvement programs helps employees develop leadership skills and positively affects their job success and future opportunities. This also provides direct communication links with management.

ASSESSING TRAINING NEEDS

Training is another method to communicate accurate information to managers, supervisors, and employees, although a good trainer will tell you that training is never needed for training's sake alone. A training program should be prepared and delivered *only* to fill a specific need.

Before any training program is established the following analysis should be conducted:

Is Training Needed?

Training is often associated with a new employee on the job, but the concept has rehabilitative value, too. When employees are not performing their jobs correctly, the problem should be reviewed to determine whether it can be solved by retraining. Problems that can be effectively remedied by training include lack of knowledge about a work process, unfamiliarity with equipment, or incorrect performance of a task.

Identify Specific Training Needs

Further study may be needed of jobs to identify exactly what employees are expected to do and in what ways they are not meeting job requirements. A job analysis that breaks down each of the steps of a job into a working procedure is a helpful technique. Such a review should result in a basic lesson plan.

Another key question is: How much knowledge about the subject do the participants already have? At what level will the training take place? For example, new information for a group of apprentices will be presented differently than a refresher training for experienced machinists in the use of maintenance shop equipment.

Set the Training Goals

Once specific training needs have been identified, what will the training activity accomplish? Clear, measurable goals should be determined as to what the employee is expected to do. Objectives should describe what constitutes acceptable performance and describe the conditions under which the individual will demonstrate competence.

Matching company training goals to the clearly identified needs of workers motivates employees to receive training information and apply it back on the job.

What Is the Best Learning Method?

How can the new information be transferred to practical application on the job? Here trainers must match learning situations with the objective of the activity so that the learning situation simulates actual job needs as closely as possible.

A variety of training techniques can be used—lecture, group discussion, interactive computer-based training, simulation, role playing, equipment demonstration, charts, diagrams, films, and video tapes. The program should allow employees to demonstrate clearly that they have learned the desired skills or knowledge that was missing when training needs were identified.

The person selected to conduct the training should be knowledgeable about the subject material, able to answer in-depth questions, and have the self-confidence to conduct training in front of a group. In some cases it will be a department supervisor, in other cases a well-trained and respected mechanic. In some situations an outsider may be hired to conduct the training.

Conduct the Training

Once the missing areas of knowledge have been identified the next step is to organize the training program into one or more lesson plans. Consideration should be given to the nature of the workplace, training resources available, the length of each training session, and the number of sessions required to cover the material.

Evaluate the Training Efforts

Supervisors' observations or the result of test scores will provide a key to effectiveness of the training. If evaluation of the program reveals that objectives were missed and employees did not achieve the level of skills expected, the training process should be reevaluated. It may be necessary to reschedule parts of the training, using the additional input to revise sections of the training materials.

Keep Good Records

Training costs money. A detailed record should be kept of training costs and who attended what sessions as a way of evaluating the expenditures. Government compliance officers will frequently inspect training records on their site visits to confirm that training was in fact conducted.

SPECIAL TRAINING NEEDS

Many workplaces have a literacy problem and don't realize that some workers can't read well—or at all—or have a hearing impairment or learning disability that hinders their ability to make sense of words and phrases.

Inability to understand job instructions can quickly result in quality problems in work performance or unsafe operation of machinery.

Few employees will admit they can't read or write well or that they have trouble understanding English. Some give the impression that they are not interested in the material when they are really trying to avoid having to read text in front of them. Some bluff their way through training sessions, hoping that the memory of what they heard will serve them well back on the job. The cultural backgrounds of some employees also may discourage the asking of questions, further contributing to the problem of understanding instructions.

"Illiteracy" is defined simply as the inability to read or write, but the word "illiterate" may involve a number of reading and learning comprehension problems, such as:

- For foreign-born workers English may not be the primary reading or speaking language, and, without training in English, these immigrants are unable to comprehend not only the meaning of written words but even some verbal instructions in English

- Persons who are deaf or who have hearing impairment problems

- Persons who have a reading disability, such as dyslexia, which hinders clear comprehension of words and sentences in reading materials

Finding Better Ways to Communicate

Communications problems are significant among American workers but can be overcome in a number of ways, all of which take time and effort on the part of management, frequently with assistance from the personnel professional. Constructive steps that can be taken include:

- ► Simplifying training materials and reducing the material to basic terms with supporting graphics and visuals.

- ► Using alternative methods of instruction including audience participation, words highlighted with graphic support, and even simple interactive computer programs.

- ► Offering classes in English as a second language for foreign-born workers.

- ► Translating meeting materials and instructions into foreign languages used by major segments of the workforce.

- ► Having other employees act as language interpreters; or, in the case of hearing impaired or deaf persons, providing sign language interpreters.

- ► Offering foreign language classes to managers, supervisors, and job instructors. Some companies that have a large number of hearing impaired or deaf employees train supervisors in the basics of sign language.

Large organizations have internal staff or use outside consultants to adapt their training materials to a multilevel audience. But the task is not so easy for small organizations.

A small Connecticut manufacturer rose to the challenge of hazard communication training by providing three sessions for employees. A training video was first presented in English, then in Spanish, using a Spanish voiceover of the same film. A third session was held for Polish-speaking workers utilizing the services of an interpreter.

Training workers to read, speak, and write in English is a low-cost investment that will pay off many times over in increased safety on the job, improved quality, productivity, and a deep sense of loyalty to the employer who invested a few dollars in the future of his employees.

TRAINING FOR PERSONS WITH SPECIAL NEEDS

An often-overlooked area of safety training is that of persons with special training needs—those who are deaf or with hearing impairments and those with learning disabilities.

Hearing Impairments

Hearing impairment affects more persons in America than any other chronic disability. Estimates vary, but as many as 22 million persons in this country are thought to experience hearing losses ranging in degree from mild to profound. Another 2 million are considered deaf and cannot hear or understand conversational speech or most environmental sounds even when amplified.

On the job there can be real safety problems when an employee has difficulty in hearing instructions or hearing approaching vehicles or alarms. Hearing protection worn in high-noise areas and carefully fitted and inserted in the ear canal can do much to slow the onset of hearing loss.

Careful job orientation and instruction is key to the safety of a hearing-impaired or deaf employee. Instructors should point out the start and stop buttons on machines, whom to contact for assistance, and where exit doors from the facility are located. When hearing-impaired or deaf persons are employed in an area, auditory signals such as sirens, doorbells, and ringing telephones should be accompanied by visual signals such as flashing lights.

To assist persons with hearing impairments, the following suggestions are offered:

Research electronic aids. An amplification device for the telephone or a hearing aid with a T-switch magnifies whatever residual hearing the person has and often supports his/her speech skills. Telecommunication devices for the deaf (a telephone device which prints out verbal messages) both in desktop and pocket-size printers, are increasingly available.

Remember the deaf person's sensitivity to noise. A noisy environment may create a barrier to communication for someone who wears a hearing aid. Efforts should be made to minimize vibrations in the work area—these distort sounds to a hearing aid making it difficult for the deaf person to concentrate. In high-noise situations in a factory setting, hearing aids may not be useful.

Assign a buddy. To ease transition for newly-hired deaf persons, employers should consider the "buddy system" to help them orient to the new job. Sign-language interpreters are sometimes used during job interviews but once the employee becomes familiar with the job they are rarely required except as sign language presenters in large group meetings.

Review emergency plans. Emergency evacuation plans for the facility should be reviewed with hearing-impaired persons. Converting a fire alarm signal to a flashing light near the hearing-impaired person is a constructive step. Also ask co-workers to assist in reminding the employee when an emergency exists.

Overcoming Learning Disabilities

The learning disabled person has difficulty in taking information through his/her senses and processing that information accurately to the brain. The problems are neurological in origin and affect both children and adults.

Dyslexia is one of the most common learning disabilities and involves difficulty in reading; *dyscalculia* is difficulty with arithmetic and mathematics. *Dysgraphia* is the inability to write. Other learning disabilities can impact a person's organizational skills or interpersonal relationships (the ability to get along with others).

Attention-deficit disorder (ADD), which is sometimes associated with learning disabilities, is a neurobiological disorder whose causes are not known. It evidences itself in short attention span, easy distractability, impulsive behavior, disorganization, and frequently hyperactivity.

Helping the Learning Disabled Employee

Relatively minor job accommodations can tap the talents and capabilities of learning disabled persons. Persons with learning disabilities should be matched with their abilities and assigned work in their areas of strength. A careful job analysis is essential for getting a good placement match.

Rehabilitation counselors can be helpful in assisting employees by assessing their strengths and finding jobs that capitalize on their strong points. Remember that the Americans with Disabilities Act requires employers to consider reasonable accommodations for individuals with disabilities, including learning disabilities, if the person is otherwise qualified for the job.

Here are a few examples of accommodations:

- ► Offering persons with a learning disorder front seats in a training class. This allows them to concentrate on the presentation.

- ► Learning disabled persons may need extra time to complete a test or examination, take an oral exam rather than written test, or be allowed to take a tape recorder to a meeting.

- ► Computer software enhancements may be required for some persons with learning disabilities who perform computer-oriented jobs.

► Effective trainers enunciate clearly, face their audiences, and use short sentences to keep attention and interest. These effective training techniques are of particular help to learning disabled persons.

► Overloading of detailed instructions from supervisors can distract individuals with learning disabilities. Some learning disabled persons carry tape recorders to capture supervisory instructions which serve as a reminder to them.

Accommodations for people with learning disabilities may require time and management skills on the part of immediate supervisors. Frequent performance feedback from their supervisor can help learning disabled persons keep on track.

ASK YOURSELF

► Should you develop an employee handbook? What should it cover?

► How will you manage the "rumor mill"?

► What kinds of training will your employees require?

► Are all of your employees literate? How do you know for certain?

► How well do you communicate negative news?

CHAPTER
NINE

DEVELOPING
PROFESSIONALISM

CHAPTER NINE

A POSITIVE IMAGE

In this chapter we deal with some of the intangible but important qualities that will help make a personnel professional successful.

Personal leadership and a positive image are key elements for success in a personnel professional's job. Keeping that demeanor is not always easy when associates and friends are involved in a workforce reduction or when trying to explain the limitations of insurance coverage to an employee with a serious illness.

Working hard to keep a positive image can make for success of the personnel professional. In today's difficult business environment that challenge is not always easily met.

Here are some thoughts to help the personnel professional maintain that positive image, even in times of adversity:

Listen a lot. People quickly tire of a motor mouth. Listening casually and tactfully will allow the personnel representative to focus on employee and fellow worker concerns. There's great therapy in letting a person talk; and it's great for the personnel professional to have a reputation as a good listener.

Don't talk—explain. After you've listened to employee concerns, try restating in the employee's own words what was said, such as, "As I understand your concern about the new job, you feel that . . ." Carefully measured responses to the employee along with good eye contact may help settle the employee concerns, or at least gain recognition for your best efforts to settle the problem.

Be courteous. A pleasant greeting, a smile, and courteous opening remarks go a long way to establish a positive impression of the personnel professional, the personnel office, and of the company.

Polish your writing and presentation skills. Good managers speak and write clearly. Know your material and be prepared to present it clearly and forcefully in the time frame allotted.

Keep a sense of humor. On more than one occasion an appropriate touch of humor has relieved a tense situation, a confrontation is defused, and the players return to work and go about their regular business.

Have compassion. Not every personnel decision is easy in today's difficult business environment, and many employees are faced with work and family responsibilities that would have put earlier generations out of action.

Practice common sense. The world of work is not a textbook world and the personnel professional won't find all the answers needed in a college textbook on human resources or in the personnel policies binder on the bookshelf. Personnel people have to use their "gut feelings" at times, along with a healthy sprinkling of old-fashioned common sense to work toward solutions to a problem that is fair to both management and employees.

Keep fit and presentable. Make a viable effort to look like someone who is upward bound.

Stay positive. Your best career asset is your positive support network—your superior, managers, co-workers and even that newly-hired employee who appreciates the job and thinks well of you. Running around with the moaners and groaners will not enhance your job image!

That may seem like a long list but it takes a special kind of person to be successful in the personnel field, one who knows what he or she is doing, can explain those concepts to others up and down the management-employee ladder, and can do it cheerfully.

Most successful people are optimistic, positive, and enthusiastic. Positive attitudes, backed by professional performance on the job, can result in a lilt of inner self-confidence that even the most negative situations won't tear down.

MANAGING THE WORK DAY

Workdays for personnel people are not always neat and orderly but a number of techniques can be employed to bring a sense of order to disruption and disarray. Here are some thoughts.

A positive impression is left when a visitor to the department sees organized desk surfaces, even if there are piles of records or paperwork on the desk. Neatly arranged and stacked files beat clutter. A multilevel file tray or rack will help organize piles of paper and get them out of the way temporarily, until they can find their way to a filing cabinet or be entered into the computer.

A multitude of telephone contacts are difficult at times to handle courteously and effectively. Identifying yourself as "Good morning, human resources, Lee Jones" will shorten the time spent on the phone and encourage clear identification from the caller.

Careful record keeping and note taking is of prime importance in a personnel office. Telephone messages that come from employees saying they will be absent, the reason for the absence, and employees who resign over the telephone become important ingredients for the employee personnel file. Good, accurate work here can make or break the effectiveness of an employer action at some time in the future.

Conscious attention to detail can help the personnel staff gain control of their work routine and present a positive, professional image to outsiders.

PREPARING YOURSELF FOR THE FUTURE

Once the personnel management function is well established where do you go from here?

In this rapidly changing world continuing professional education is the name of the game. Professionals in personnel management will want to keep themselves up-to-date by attending seminars and workshops in personnel and human resource management and stay current by reading professional journals in the field.

Continuing education is important for the personnel professional to keep up on evolving trends in the field. Many companies have tuition refund plans which reimburse employees for higher education courses upon successful completion of the course. Many of these courses give out CEU's—Continuing Education Units—at completion providing a permanent record of the educational accomplishments of the person.

New developments in computer software are arriving on the market every day to help the personnel professional make their jobs more efficient and the results more exact.

Professional Certification

The Human Resource Certification Institute is part of SHRM (Society for Human Resource Management), the leading professional organization in the field. The Institute schedules certification tests at many locations around the country three times a year to examine the test takers' understanding of the body of knowledge of the human resources profession. A certification study guide is available from the Institute as well as more professional and senior-level learning systems in the human resources field.

Successful exam takers may achieve the designation of Professional in Human Resources (PHR) or the more advanced Senior Professional in Human Resources (SPHR).

ASK YOURSELF

► Where do you go from here?

► What do you feel are the five most important qualities of a personnel professional?

CHAPTER
TEN

PULLING
IT ALL
TOGETHER

THE HR FUNCTION

Personnel management is a staff function to serve the line organization and other departments in the organization. Its clients are line managers and supervisors, the managers of other staff departments, and the employee workforce. We began with this basic maxim at the start of this book, and we reaffirm it here.

The human resources function does not exist as a free-standing entity. Internal clients are no different from the external customers that a sales representative deals with.

Clients of the human resources function have specific needs and expectations. Hopefully they gain value from the services provided by the personnel function. These clients have every right to quality and service, provided cheerfully, and on time.

As satisfying as human resources work may be at times, it is not an end in itself. Personnel professionals are employed to make the organization more successful— to help the company produce better products or offer enhanced services.

GETTING YOUR MANAGER TO LISTEN

Getting your immediate supervisor to listen to your professional problems is not always an easy task. Busy, upper-level managers have many items vying for their attention— production problems, quality complaints, and financial performance. A personnel problem may not be a high priority with them.

Personnel professionals should keep the following practices in mind when communicating with their immediate supervisor:

► Find out how your boss likes to receive information— through face-to-face contact with you, through memos, telephone calls, or staff meetings—or all of the above? Determine the best method(s) for communicating effectively with your superior.

► Unless it is an emergency, pick your time and place to communicate with your boss. Try to avoid his or her busy times of the day. Pick times where your supervisor is more likely to be tuned in to you and your needs.

► Don't ramble—get right to the point. State your case succinctly. Don't outline a problem unless you have either a recommendation or a solution that you have implemented. Bosses don't like "dumpers"—professionals who drop the problem in their laps and expect the boss to have the answer.

There's nothing wrong with asking your boss' opinion about one or more avenues of approach or potential solutions to the problem but do your homework first—be sure you have analyzed the problem to the best of your ability and developed potential solutions.

► When a new work assignment is routed to you, be sure you understand where the project fits into your boss's priorities and the business's short- and long-term goals.

► If your boss feels strongly about an approach that you disagree with, ask politely for an explanation and point out some of the disadvantages—presuming you've done your research and can back up your position with facts.

► If you are not sure of an item, back off and ask for more time to check into the problem. Return with your facts and recommendations and go at it again.

► And when you do a good job and receive compliments from others, don't assume your boss is aware of the accomplishments. Find a low-key way to make your supervisor aware of good work.

A good working relationship with your boss is important to success for both of you. Building a positive and effective working relationship with your supervisor means understanding his or her work methods and style.

DELEGATING

How do personnel professionals get the job done when there are bulges in the workload? There are ways to handle some of the overload and still see that the job gets done.

Share the load. Personnel professionals may not be able to do everything asked of them, but they may be able to guide, coordinate, and facilitate an activity. For example, take an annual event such as the company picnic, an assignment that often falls into the lap of a personnel person. That responsibility can be shared with others by forming an employee committee to plan and run the affair—one person assigned to ticket sales, another to run games and activities, a third to coordinate food arrangements, and so on.

Before a personnel professional leaves work, try to line up the important projects for the next workday. Then prioritize them (1, 2, 3, etc.). Tackle the demanding projects when you are freshest and at your best—perhaps early in the work day.

Get others to do the jobs they are being paid to do. Some persons, including supervisors, would have personnel people do their work for them. Personnel people should gently push the responsibility back where it belongs—to the appropriate manager.

HANDLING INTERRUPTIONS

The work life of a personnel person is not likely to be smooth and uninterrupted. Personnel people don't work behind closed doors on research projects and rarely are they able to shut out interactions with other persons for long periods of time. In fact, an effective personnel person thrives on interaction with other people at all levels in the organization. Interruptions are part of the job of a personnel professional and must be handled courteously.

Allow time in your workday for these necessary interactions, but when you must work for a period of time without interruption, here are some suggestions:

- ▶ Go behind closed doors for the period of time you need. Use an unoccupied conference room or a spare office. Perhaps a day working at home is needed. But be sure to shut the office door to show that it is something special that you are working on.

- ▶ If people still want to see you, schedule an appointment for a time after you have finished the project.

- ▶ And for the talkers and chronic interrupters you may have to set some stiff rules to demonstrate that you are a busy business person. Politely encourage persons to make appointments with you or go see them on their turf—perhaps in their office where you can regulate the amount of time you spend there.

Being assertive and realistic about time is the hallmark of a professional. Most of your colleagues will respect you for it.

OBTAINING FEEDBACK

Like any employee, personnel professionals need feedback to know how their "product" is being received and how effective they are in their work.

The personnel professional should be direct and ask for feedback on how he or she is doing. Listen carefully to what people say. If they believe you are genuinely interested and sincere, they'll likely offer suggestions to improve performance or compliment work that has been done well.

Ask how you can make your work more exact, more thorough, more acceptable. Can you discontinue activities that are not meaningful to your client in the line organization or in another staff department? You'll be pleasantly surprised how dedicated attention to a problem can result in marked improvement.

Improvement to service is not a program, but rather a *process*. Programs have a starting and ending point but a process of offering a quality service is ongoing.

Your Turn

► How *are* you doing? If you have an established personnel management program, reflect on any feedback you have received. If you haven't received any, think of what you can do to find out.

COMPUTER APTITUDE

Computers first entered the world of personnel management through human resource information systems. Computer use has now spread rapidly so that information storage and retrieval is now involved in benefits and compensation administration, recruiting and testing, and in communication and interactive training activities.

These days the personnel professional *must* have computer knowledge and expertise. Computers are on the desks of more and more human resource managers and professionals. Lack of knowledge of computers and their potential in human resources management can be associated with lack of professionalism.

International networks of computers, including the Internet, are opening new doors and opportunities, especially in recruitment, for human resources professionals who have the equipment and mindset to venture into this arena.

Your Turn

► What is the computer proficiency of the personnel profession at your business? Is it where it should be?

PROFESSIONAL LIABILITY

Managers of all types, including human resource managers, are routinely named these days as defendants in government charges or court cases filed by disgruntled present and former employees.

As a result some managers, including human resource professionals, are being held personally liable by some courts for their own acts of discrimination and are also being held liable for the acts of other managers and workers of which the managers have knowledge. Such incidents are rare but are rising in our litigious society.

For example, Title VII of the Civil Rights Act of 1964 prohibits employers from discriminating based on race, color, religion, sex, or national origin. The term "employer" includes someone with 15 or more employees and any "agent" of that person, which includes managers and supervisors of the employer. The Fair Labor Standards Act (FLSA) defines an employer very broadly to include any person "acting directly or indirectly in the interest of the employer in relation to the employee." That broad definition would also include most managers and supervisors.

Insurance coverage in most businesses provides protection for officers and agents but insurance does not usually cover any intentional acts, punitive damages, or criminal liability. If the manager is acting outside his or her duties, the insurance coverage may not apply. Criminal liability is generally based on a reckless disregard for safety and not mere negligence. If a manager intentionally ignores warning signs, he or she can be held to have a reckless disregard.

There are also a number of state statutes, some of which hold criminal penalties. For example, in many states, a terminated employee is entitled to final wages on the next business day after termination—*not* on the next regular payday. Although payment at termination will often require a deviation from the regular payroll schedule, failure to do so is an offense in some states.

Some states require that newly-hired employees be informed in writing of their rate of pay, hours of work, and wage payment schedule at the time of hire. Large employers pretty well have this in hand but small businesses often find themselves in violation of this statute.

Personnel managers need not be lawyers but they must understand what legal requirements exist and what can happen in litigation.

ESTABLISHING PRIORITIES—A CASE STUDY

One of the first tasks that a business manager or a newly appointed personnel manager has to tackle is deciding "What comes first?"

Often business managers have very definite ideas of what needs to be managed early in the game—problem areas that have not been handled well under an informal personnel structure. A professional personnel person, after a few weeks on the job, will also have some ideas of what needs to be improved, better coordinated, dropped or added to existing activities.

An Example from an Expanding Business

The following analysis of personnel priorities was developed by a newly appointed personnel manager at a New York state manufacturing plant with 95 employees. Expansion of the existing facility was planned and another new plant was in the offing for Texas within two years.

The existing personnel structure consisted of a payroll clerk who also handled some personnel responsibilities. The plant manager and five shift supervisors picked up, in various ways, the remaining personnel responsibilities. The plant is nonunion.

The President of the company felt these were early priorities in the formalized personnel management function:

► Better organize the employment process and reduce turnover which was slowing production and delaying expansion

► Get a better safety program underway to cut down on accidents, stave off OSHA inspections, and get control of mounting workers compensation costs

► Foster the owner's concept of a close working relationship with employees and a management responsive to employee concerns and needs

► Be involved in planning for the future staffing needs of the second plant

Here is how the personnel manager developed priorities and approached the new responsibilities:

Week One

- Meet with the president, plant manager, and each of the supervisors

- Meet with the payroll/personnel clerk

- Introduce self to every employee

- Review existing recruitment activities

- Review file of OSHA citations and obtain background on current safety activities

Remaining Weeks of the First Month

Discuss existing hiring activities in detail with personnel clerk. Meet with plant manager and supervisors to gain their input on present recruitment program and areas that need improvement. Review turnover statistics and reasons for separations.

Meet with manager of state job service office. Meet job counselor assigned to the company and invite for a tour of the facility.

Based on input from personnel clerk and supervisors:

- review existing new hire orientation program (none) — PRIORITY

- need to forecast hiring needs with more lead time — PLANT MANAGER

- pre-employment substance abuse and post-offer medical exam procedure (none) — PRIORITY

- redefine need to match job needs with candidates; too much "stand up" interviewing by supervisors. Supervisors not interviewing all candidates — PLANT MANAGER

Sales department needs to expand and add more field sales reps; meet with sales manager, sales office supervisor, and a sales representative to understand nature of the work. Develop employment advertisement for additional sales representatives and conduct screening to present final candidates to sales manager.

Review unemployment compensation reports—in disarray and some claims not challenged. Work with personnel clerk to set up a review system to respond promptly to claims and challenge those where statements disagree with our facts. — PRIORITY

Several employees approach with job-related complaints. Ask why they don't go to the supervisor—don't have confidence in several supervisors. Discuss with plant manager; need to reaffirm an in-house appeals process, emphasizing that supervisor is the first person an employee should speak to about a job-related problem. — PRIORITY

Month Two

Increasing concern about effective supervision in place; need for consistent and uniform treatment of employees. Need to have an appeals process, supported by supervision. Need to have a working session with supervisors (Saturday morning) to develop an appeals structure and a uniform discipline policy. Need to discuss how supervisors communicate with their employees on work direction, company policies, controversial items? Do employees feel that they can register a complaint without retaliation?

PRIORITY

Assess safety committee activity. Going well despite a number of accidents, but not high in relationship to manufacturing industry. Excessive focus on unsafe working conditions when most of the accidents are being caused by unsafe work practices. Attend meetings and support existing activity. Get plant manager or a respected supervisor to chair safety committee. Advise President that present safety activity needs only fine-tuning.

Discuss with plant manager methods of communication with employees. This is a small business, plant manager reminds. Uses one-on-one from supervisor to employee and letters on notice board. Suggest regular crew meetings to communicate information and allow employees opportunity to ask questions. OK with plant manager if supervisors agree. Indifferent reception from supervisors.

PRIORITY

Month Three

Since the company has contracts with the federal government, develop company policy statement on affirmative action, nondiscrimination and sexual harassment. No affirmative action programs (AAP) developed yet, although workforce has a good mix of women and minorities. Develop AAP in second six months.

Discuss usefulness of policy manual or employee handbook. Premature. Little interest at this time as most contacts are informal, but resulting in inconsistencies in treatment of employees.

A number of employee complaints about incentives; sort out incentives problem and start work on an easily understood and equitable policy. Work with controller.   PRIORITY

Review merit rating system with supervisors; correct paperwork failures and get merit rating system operational for every merit increase. Without supporting paperwork no merit increase will be processed.   PRIORITY

Months Four Five, and Six

Review attendance control procedure with supervisors (needs improvement); gain input and present revised procedure to supervisors for their approval—and use. Publicize and get absence control procedure effective first of next month.

Formalize probationary or orientation period of 45 days for new factory hires. Require written evaluation of new hires no later than the 40th day.

Restructure personnel function to bring recruiting, interviewing, and recommendation-to-hire activities fully within personnel function. Advance notice of hiring still needs some improvement but try to develop pool of prospective new hires.

Review employment application form and other employment forms for legal acceptability. Review notice board postings to meet government requirements.

Assure that every employment file has an acceptable I–9 form.

Develop and publish an hourly employee length-of-service list so that supervisors can give more consideration to company length of service.

Start formal exit interviews for terminating employees. We need to know, to the best of our ability, why employees are leaving. (Early indications are that labor and machine operator rates are competitive but mechanics rates are low in the community.)   PRIORITY

Conduct mini survey of benchmark rates through chamber of commerce. Hire-on rates are competitive but mechanics rates are 10–20 percent below community. Recommend changes to mechanics rate structure to plant manager and president effective first of next month.

Complaints about vending service and food pricing in the canteen. Form employee committee to work on problem. Meet with present supplier; unsatisfactory response. Give vendor two months to improve and, in meantime, obtain quotations from other prospective vendors.

Review with supervisors the concept of Standards of Conduct (plant rules) and ask for their help in developing SCs. Supervisors suggest employee committee be asked to make recommendations for work rules. What are most serious infractions—leaving premises without permission, walking off the job, unreported for X days. Committee set up to develop revised set of rules with completion date two months hence.

Review first aid system. Need more formalized system, training of additional first aid attendants, and refresher training for supervisors and present   PRIORITY attendants. Need better relationship with occupational medicine clinic nearby. As a result of complaints from night shift, review medical clinic hiring exam procedures and accident treatment procedures.

Review status of personal protective equipment in use. Plant safety committee offers to do this. Due to a large number of minor eye injuries, reassess what jobs require safety eyeglasses.   **PRIORITY**

Review fringe benefits. Clarify vacation pay policy as more than half employees "buy" their vacation time and do not take time off. Large number of absences day before and day after a holiday; nail down holiday payment requirements.

Plant manager complains that employees are not carrying out specific instructions of supervisors and wants to discipline. Discuss present methods of communication which plant manager now agrees need improvement. Take plant manager to a state manufacturer's association seminar on communications. He's impressed and wants all his supervisors to attend. Offer to coach each supervisor in developing initial crew meeting formats. First crew meetings scheduled for following week.

Personal leaves of absences granted for many requests; loosely managed. Employees return to work without advance notice resulting in overstaffing in some departments.

President and plant manager coming around to necessity of having written policies and procedures to guide supervisors; review existing policies and letters for compliance to federal and state law. Review page by page at a supervisors' meeting and issue. Next, finalize the company's Standards of Conduct; publicize and distribute internally.   **PRIORITY**

Review coverages and costs of present medical plan. Obtain data through chamber of commerce and recommend adjustments to plan effective for first of year. Prepare advance publicity, new explanatory materials, and revised SPDs (Summary Plan Descriptions).

With six months experience in recruitment, develop a Selection Standards profile for frequently recruited plant and office jobs which will allow recruiting best possible candidates.   PRIORITY

Assure that employment and selection standards meet applicable regulations—checking of references to be upgraded and formalized.

Begin use of a patent and secrecy agreement for mechanics and professional and managerial employees.

Focus on training and development needs of each supervisor (in past six months one has quit and a second asked to return to mechanic status) and key staff and office members and develop training and development plan for ensuing year. Scout for potential supervisory candidates for Plant 2 which will be operational within two years.

Focus on training and development needs for key plant hourlys and develop training outline to overcome deficiencies.

Recommend educational assistance/tuition refund plan.

Clarify job roles—we expect mechanics to direct employees working on machines in their area.

Offer and encourage immigrant employees to enroll in English as a Second Language course. Consider bonus or award for successful completion.

Develop model affirmative action program for the facility; review draft copy with plant manager and supervisors for their input and commitment to achieve goals and timetables.

Review plant's compliance with applicable federal and state safety regulations—Right-to-Know, MSDS, noise control and hearing conservation, safety eyewear, personal protective equipment, etc. Use outside loss-control consultant to do training.

PRIORITY

Assess services from workers' compensation carrier and, if needed, direct improvement.

LONGER-
TERM

In a growing company explore possibilities of employee involvement in the business to as high a degree as they are capable of and interested in. The concept has application in productivity, quality improvement, equipment improvement, customer contact and relationships, safety, and workers' compensation control.

Develop and finalize incentive plan that will give full consideration to productivity, quality, reruns, and returns from customers and considers changing conditions, new equipment, and employee efficiency.

With help from a committee of mechanics and supervisors, develop written mechanic training program that will focus on basic training and the needs of this business. Explore possible application of a formal apprenticeship program. Develop written operator training program.

. . . And so it goes. Priorities are juggled as the needs of the business dictate. At times the list of priorities seems overwhelming but this personnel manager was able to give attention to the hot spots first, and then, with input from the line organization, developed personnel programs that were later embraced.

And . . . The Future

In the opening chapter of this book we reminded personnel professionals that they are there to assist the line organization in carrying out its mainstream role of manufacturing a product or offering a service—and helping make a profit for the organization.

A personnel management function does not exist in its own right or because somebody thinks it is a good idea. It is there to enhance the profit of the business as it grows. A personnel professional with knowledge of the techniques of the personnel field, high motivation, enthusiasm, and presentation skills can help enhance profitability of the business and their own careers.

ASK YOURSELF

► How will you handle the many interruptions that are common to the personnel function?

► What will be the measurement of your effectiveness in the personnel function?

► Think of three things you can do that will improve your ability to streamline the personnel management function.

► What are your top three priorities for your personnel manager to tackle?

APPENDIXES

Appendix I
Job Responsibilities

What do personnel people do? The best way to show the broad and varied duties of personnel managers, professionals, and support staff is to illustrate with some job descriptions from typical personnel jobs. These responsibilities and duties will vary from business to business, depending on the size and needs of the organization. Here is a sampling.

Personnel Assistant

A nonexempt position that provides administrative and human resources assistance to human resource managers or administrative managers.

Reports to: Personnel Manager

Duties and Responsibilities:

1. Answers routine inquires from supervisors and employees on employment verifications, benefits questions, and job openings. Screens incoming telephone calls; handles within scope of responsibilities and refers other calls to manager for handling.

2. Fills requisitions for temporary personnel from designated local employment agency as needed. Greets temporary personnel and escorts them to assigned manager.

3. Maintains employment resumes, application forms, and applicant flow logs in line with company policy. Advises state job service of open jobs and forwards classified advertisements to local newspapers. Sorts responses to advertisements.

4. Verifies unemployment insurance claims and refers exceptions to personnel manager for review. Advises terminating employees of COBRA coverages and processes applications for continued insurance coverage.

5. Maintains employee personnel files in line with company policies and government regulations. Retains records in accordance with company record retention requirements.

6. Provides human resources department orientation on company policies and programs for new hires; signs up new employees for various programs. Escorts new employee to supervisor.

7. Maintains plant and office bulletin boards in an up-to-date and legal compliance manner.

8. Answers questions from employees on benefit plan provisions and assists in resolving problems with the insurance carrier.

9. Subs for the employment interviewer during vacations or absence and assists during heavy hiring periods.

Qualifications:

1. Ability to maintain the highly confidential nature of human resources work.

2. At least two years college or equivalent business experience, including courses in human resources management.

3. At least two years administrative or human resources experience.

4. Personal computer and word processing skills.

5. Tact, above-average communication skills, and ability to work effectively both with employees and managers. Ability to convey a positive and professional image to applicants and employees.

Employment Supervisor

Coordinates recruiting and staffing activity of the company, including internal and external recruitment and placement, college recruiting—consistent with the company's commitment as an equal opportunity employer.

Reports to: Manager Human Resources

1. Develops recruitment and placement policies, systems, and procedures to meet the company's employment needs. Reviews and approves all exempt employment advertisements. Negotiates employment fee structures with major placement agencies.

2. Directs recruitment activities of the company, including university and college recruiting, masters' level recruitment, and outplacement centers for armed forces officers.

3. Upon determination of recruiting needs, reviews promotional slates and personnel files of likely candidates within the company. Refers files of qualified persons to hiring supervisor for review.

4. For external recruiting, uses a job description for the open job and develops a recruiting specification for approval of hiring supervisor. Determines most logical recruiting methods to attract candidates.

5. Develops advertisements for open positions and places ads in most effective media. Contacts college placement offices and alumni offices. With approval of supervisor may select a placement agency to assist in recruitment process.

6. Conducts interviews and recommends semifinal candidates to hiring managers. Scouts for persons who may be suitable for other openings in the company.

7. Assists in special affirmative action recruitment programs as they relate to the hiring of women, minorities, veterans, or individuals with disabilities.

8. Acts as liaison in dealings with federal and state agencies and with special interest groups.

9. Organizes and conducts training programs in effective employment interviewing, consistent with current laws and regulations and provisions of the Americans with Disabilities Act.

10. Manages the company's college relations program and maintains positive professional relationships with college and alumni placement staffs.

Qualifications:

1. Bachelor's degree, or equivalent, in human resources management or business. Advanced degree or an MBA a plus.

2. Extensive interviewing experience (at least five years) for exempt candidates for positions in a manufacturing company.

3. Excellent interviewing skills. Must have a thorough knowledge of recruitment and selection techniques and requirements of the federal Selection Guidelines and the Americans with Disabilities Act.

4. Willingness to travel extensively in recruiting activity.

5. Platform skills allowing effective presentations to students and faculty; excellent interpersonal skills to interact effectively with recruiting officials and applicants.

Supervisor Employee and Labor Relations

Provides leadership and counsel on company policies involving employee and labor relations, compliance issues such as affirmative action, EEO and safety and health, and workers' compensation matters.

Reports to: Human Resource Manager

Duties and Responsibilities:

1. Provides guidance to field locations in the handling of lay-offs, staff reduction, termination of employees with more than two years' service, and local employee relations issues.

2. Assists plants with interpretation of labor agreement contract language, acts as the company representative at third-step grievances and presents company's case at arbitration.

3. Reviews developments in safety, occupational health, and worker' compensation issues. Advises plants of changes which affect them and develops management and employee awareness training programs as necessary on new regulations.

4. Acts as the company's ranking representative in dealing with federal agencies such as OSHA, EEOC, etc. Coordinates presentation of company's position to these agencies on individual charges or complaints.

5. Manages resolution of problem workers' compensation claims and reviews and approves all settlement offers in workers' compensation cases. Coordinates contacts with loss-control service organizations and workers' compensation carriers.

6. Develops model affirmative action plans for the company and reviews completed plans at each location for acceptability to government requirements and company policy.

7. Reviews new and revised job descriptions from industrial engineering department to assure compliance with company policy, government compliance requirements, including Americans with Disabilities Act.

8. Attends quarterly manufacturing management meetings as employee relations department representative and annual sales, distribution, and R & D meetings.

Qualifications:

1. Four-year degree in human resource management, law, or general business.

2. At least five years' experience as a plant human resource manager in a unionized environment.

3. Strong, persuasive skills to explain company position to diverse groups of employees.

The following position descriptions are provided courtesy of the Society for Human Resource Management, Alexandria, Virginia.

Human Resources Manager

1. Develops and administers various human resources plans and procedures for company personnel.

2. Plans, organizes, and controls all activities of the department. Participates in developing department goals, objectives, and systems.

3. Implements and annually updates compensation program; rewrites job descriptions as necessary; conducts annual salary surveys, and develops merit pool (salary budget); analyzes compensation; monitors performance evaluation program and revises as necessary.

4. Develops, recommends, and implements personnel policies and procedures; prepares and maintains handbooks on policies and procedures; performs benefit administration to include claims resolution, change reporting, approving invoices for payment, annual re-evaluation of policies for cost effectiveness, information activities, and cash flow.

5. Develops and maintains affirmative action program; files EEO-1 annually; maintains other records, reports, and logs to conform to EEO regulations.

6. Conducts recruitment effort for all exempt and nonexempt personnel, students, and temporary employees; conducts new employee orientations, monitors career path program, employee relations counseling, outplacement counseling, and exit interviewing; writes and places employment advertisements.

7. Establishes and maintains department records and reports. Participates in administrative staff meetings and attends other meetings, such as seminars. Maintains company organization charts and employee directory.

8. Evaluates reports and decisions in relation to established goals. Recommends new approaches, policies, and procedures to effect continual improvement in efficiency of department and services performed.

9. Performs other incidental and related duties as required and assigned.

Knowledge and Skills:

1. Equivalent to appropriate four-year college program

2. Responsible for human resources planning and development

3. Provides functional guidance for administrative support needs

Education and Work Experience:

A bachelor's degree and five years' human resource experience or a master's degree in human resource management and four years' experience in the HR field or nine years' experience in the HR field or any appropriate combination of education and experience.

Training Manager

Provides a service within the organization and implements all training programs. The programs would include but are not limited to quality control, work measurement, human resources, manufacturing methods, and supervisory development.

Duties and Responsibilities:

1. Develops, writes and coordinates training manuals working with specialists for specific details. The training manuals should include course content, visual charts, videotapes, slides, etc. Types initial and/or final draft of materials.

2. Prepares training videotapes and/or films; maintains library of video and film training aids. Schedules training sessions within individual training programs ensuring facility and audiovisual setup and employee notification.

3. Handles introduction of topic specialists at the start of training sessions and provides courses in such a way as to stimulate and motivate attendees. Develops a means of measuring the effectiveness of divisional training programs through testing, etc.

4. Overviews the effectiveness of programs developed and administered.

5. Develops higher skills from the existing workforce.

Education and Work Experience:

1. College level degree in one or more of the following: Human resources development, Communications, Personnel Relations, Business administration, or Teaching.

2. Minimum two years' prior training, teaching, or related human resources experience.

3. Creative ability; writing proficiency.

4. Good organizer, meticulous and good public speaker at ease moderating large groups.

Here is another perspective of the job of personnel manager—an advertisement for a personnel director in a New Jersey newspaper:

Personnel Director

Local manufacturing company seeks a personnel professional to lead its human resource activity.

The Director is responsible for overseeing design and implementation of personnel and employment policies, labor relations and legal and governmental employment issues.

Candidates should have a college degree, significant personnel management experience, excellent interpersonal and communication skills and demonstrated leadership abilities with experience in the following areas: labor relations, collective bargaining, managerial experience with union and nonunion employees, working knowledge of affirmative action plans, benefits management, workers' compensation, unemployment compensation and federal labor law.

Please submit resume and salary history to . . .

Appendix II
Federal Employment Laws

A brief outline of principal federal workplace legislation and executive orders which affect management and employees follows below, with information on the scope of coverage of the law or the threshold (minimum level) of employment to which the particular act applies. Personnel managers should possess complete copies of these laws for easy reference.

The personnel professional should understand the coverage of the law, the enforcement agency involved, any exemptions from the law, the range of penalties, and the statute of limitations for applicants—present or former employees—to file a claim.

Laws change frequently and court decisions give new emphasis or shades of meaning to existing laws. The watchword for the personnel professional should be: Stay informed of developments!

Here are highlights of the principal federal laws and regulations governing the employment relationship:

Davis Bacon Act 1931

For bidders seeking government construction contracts, the law authorizes the department of labor to establish "prevailing" wage and fringe benefits schedules for commercial construction work.

National Labor Relations Act 1935 and Amendments

Also known as the Wagner Act, workers are guaranteed broad rights to organize and bargain collectively with their employer or to engage in concerted activities such as strikes and picketing. The act prohibits employer domination of unions, bans employment discrimination to discourage union membership and a refusal to bargain in good faith.

Fair Labor Standards Act 1938 (FLSA) and Amendments

This comprehensive federal law is frequently known as the "Wage and Hour Law" and sets minimum wage standards at the federal level for employers engaged in interstate commerce. The law requires recordkeeping of hours worked and wages paid and requires payment of overtime for nonexempt employees who work more than 40 hours per week. Establishes exemptions—executive, administrative, professional, and outside sales—from overtime and minimum wage coverages. Applies to all employers engaged in interstate commerce which is very broadly defined. (Note that some states have wage and hour laws that provide benefits greater than the federal law.)

Equal Pay Act 1963 with Additions and Amendments

The act prohibits employers from paying workers of one sex less than the rate received by those of the opposite sex for jobs substantially similar or identical in skill, effort, and responsibility and performed under similar work conditions. The act applies to employers engaged in intrastate commerce and subject to Fair Labor Standards (FLSA).

Civil Rights Act (CRA) 1964 and Amendments

The law prohibits discrimination in compensation, terms and conditions of employment because of race, religion, color, sex, or national origin. Applies to private-sector employers of 15 or more workers who are employed 20 or more weeks per year.

Equal Employment Opportunity Act (EEO) 1964 and Executive Order 11246

Empowers the Equal Employment Opportunity Commission (EEOC) with the right to sue employers who are found to have discriminated against employees or applicants. The executive order requires employers with federal government contracts in excess of $10,000 a year to take positive steps to eliminate employment barriers to women and minorities.

Federal contractors or subcontractors with 50 or more employees and contracts of more than $50,000 must prepare written affirmative action plans that include goals and timetables to remedy deficiencies in the employment of women and minorities in the organization.

Age Discrimination in Employment Act (ADEA) 1967

This act prohibits employment discrimination against persons age 40 and over in hiring, promotion, demotion, compensation, transfer, and other terms and conditions of employment. The Act applies to employers with 20 or more workers in each of the 20 or more calendar weeks of the present or preceding year.

Fair Credit Reporting Act 1970

Employers are permitted to use credit data to evaluate job applicants and candidates for promotion. Requires employers to inform applicants by written notice that an inquiry into the applicant's financial status will take place and then, if denied employment because of information obtained during the inquiry, the applicant must be informed of the third party who conducted the investigation.

Occupational Safety and Health Act (OSHA) 1970

The act sets mandatory standards for safety and health for all employers in general industry, construction, maritime operations, and agriculture. Under the Act, states are permitted to develop their own safety and health adminis-tration and standards as long as the standards are as effective as the federal regulations. About half the states have chosen to have their own state-level OSH administration instead of federal coverage.

The Act also includes a General Duty Clause, Section 5(a)(1), which requires employers to operate a place of employment free from recognized hazards which are likely to cause serious injury or a fatality.

Requires posting of the yellow OSHA information poster and, employers with 11 or more employees in most industries are required to maintain a log of job injuries and illnesses and, for the month of February each year, post on a facility notice board the summary section of the OSHA Log of Work Injuries and Illnesses.

Rehabilitation Act 1973

This act prohibits discrimination by contractors who have business with the federal government totaling $2,500 or more. Employers with contracts of $50,000 or more and over 50 employees must prepare an affirmative action plan to comply with the act, although goals and timetables are not required in the plan.

Privacy Act 1974

Applies only to federal agencies and prevents them from revealing specified information to outsiders without approval of the employee.

Employee Retirement Security Act (ERISA) 1974

Where employers provide benefit plans for employees, requires employers to inform their workers about specified details of the pension and other benefit plans. Provides controls and vesting standards for pension plans and sets a base standard of funding that assures an adequate financial condition of the plan.

Vietnam-Era Veterans Readjustment Act (VEVRA) 1974

Requires federal contractors and subcontractors with business of $10,000 or more with the federal government to take affirmative action to hire and promote disabled veterans and Vietnam veterans. These employers must list job openings paying up to $25,000 with the state job service. Employers with 50 or more employees and federal contracts of at least $50,000 are required to prepare written affirmative action plans to improve the hiring and advancement of veterans, although no goals and timetables for hiring are required under the plan.

Uniform Guidelines on Employee Selection Practices 1978

This is an addendum to the Civil Rights Act and Title VII. Selection policies and practices that have an adverse impact on employment opportunities of any race, sex, or ethnic group are considered to be discriminatory, unless they can be justified by business necessity. If the selection rate for a protected group is less than four-fifths of that for the group with the highest selection rate, the selection activity is considered discriminatory unless justified by business need.

Pregnancy Discrimination Act 1978

This is another amendment to Title VII of the Civil Rights Act of 1964 and requires employers to provide pregnant employees with the same benefits as persons with any other temporary disability.

Sexual Harassment Guidelines of Title VII 1981

Employers are required to maintain an environment free of sexual harassment. Unlawful sexual harassment can arise when a supervisor requests submission to sexual advances as a condition for favorable treatment in the workplace or penalizes workers for spurning advances. Also, an employer who permits a hostile atmosphere in the workplace may be liable for harassment conduct whether or not there are victims of harassment.

Immigration Reform and Control Act (IRCA) of 1986

This act requires U.S. employers of four or more workers to complete an I-9 form on new hires requiring specific documentation from new hires to prove that they are authorized to work in the United States.

Employee Polygraph Protection Act 1988

Prohibits the use of polygraph tests and other mechanical and electrical testing mechanisms by employers engaged in interstate commerce, except in rare circumstances. Employers may administer such tests during an ongoing investigation of financial loss, assuming reasonable suspicion of the employee's guilt. Exempted from the law are private security services, employers who manufacture, distribute, or dispense controlled substances; employers engaged in intelligence and counterintelligence operations, and federal, state, and local government employees.

Drug-Free Workplace Act 1988

Employers who have contracts with the federal government of $25,000 or more must certify that they maintain a drug-free workplace by developing policies prohibiting the unlawful manufacture, distribution, possession, or use of controlled substances in the workplace; specifying actions which will be taken against those who violate the policy, including referral to a drug rehabilitation agency or termination; and providing a copy of the policy to all employees.

Worker Adjustment and Retraining Notification Act (WARN) 1988

Requires employers with 100 or more employees to give 60-day advance notice of a plant closing or a mass lay-off affecting 50 or more employees, or a lay-off affecting one-third of the work force at a given site within a 30-day period.

Older Workers' Benefit Protection Act 1990

Prohibits discrimination in employee benefits and covers all employee benefits for older workers where the employer provides such benefits.

Americans with Disabilities Act (ADA) 1990

Prohibits discrimination against qualified individuals with a disability in employment, public services and transportation, public accommodations and telecommunications. Under the Act a disability is defined as a mental or physical condition that substantially limits a major life activity. Employers, on request, are required to provide qualified individuals with disabilities with reasonable accommodations to assist them in performing the essential functions of the job, unless the accommodation would cause undue (financial) hardship to the employer. The act applies to all employers with 15 or more workers.

Substance abuse screens may be applied at any time in the selection process but employment physical examinations may not be conducted until a conditional offer of employment has been made.

Family and Medical Leave Act (FMLA) 1993

Applies to all private, state, and federal employers with 50 or more employees working within 75 miles of a given workplace. To be eligible an employee must have worked at least 12 months for the employer and worked 1,250 hours in the past year.

Eligible employees are entitled to up to a total of 12 weeks leave during any 12-month period for the birth of a child, placement of a child for adoption or foster care, serious health condition of the employee, or caring for a spouse, child, or parent with a serious health condition.

Upon return from the leave the employee is entitled to the same job or another job with equal status and pay. During the leave the employer must continue the employee's health benefits.

Appendix III
Measurement Formulas

Many managers will be satisfied to have feedback from their clients on how well—or not so well—they are doing. But not every line manager is willing to accept broad, subjective statements. Often a statistical approach will be helpful to focus on what savings—if any—are being achieved through a personnel activity.

Many line managers want statistics, which measure a return on their investment in a personnel function. Here's where personnel professionals must learn to quantify the extent of their contribution to the business.

When these basics are gathered early in the creation of a personnel function they become a helpful measuring stick in future years of the achievements of the personnel activity.

Outlined below are a number of statistical measurements of some typical personnel management activities:

Absenteeism

An absenteeism percentage is designed to measure the average rate of absence of employees and can be calculated with the following formula:

$$\frac{\text{Days lost}}{\text{Average \# of employees} \times \text{Days available}} \times 100 = \text{Absentee rate per month}$$

Example: A factory with an average of 50 employees last month had a total of 75 days of absence. The plant operated for 20 work days last month. Therefore,

$$\frac{75}{50 \times 20} \times 100 [7500 / 1,000] = 7.5\% \text{ Absentee rate last month}$$

Staff Turnover Rate

The number of voluntary (quits) and involuntary separations (layoffs, disciplinary terminations, etc.) is helpful information to compare trends over time of the percentage of employees leaving. The turnover rate can be calculated as follows:

$$\frac{\text{\# Separations during the period}}{\text{Average \# employees during the period}} \times 100 = \text{Turnover rate}$$

Example: A customer service organization with 40 employees lost 8 employees last year through voluntary quits. There were no involuntary terminations. Therefore, the turnover rate is

$$\frac{8}{40} \times 100 \ [800 \ / \ 40] = 20\% \text{ Turnover rate}$$

Cost Per Hire

Although the numbers are less precise, a "cost per hire" can be developed by considering the following information:

- Percentage of personnel department staff time spent in these recruiting activities
- Cost of medical examinations and drug screenings
- Cost of employment tests
- Cost of travel and accommodation to bring out-of-town candidates in for interviews

Then, divide the total by the number of hires.

Example: An engineering and technical services company of 50 employees hired two engineers last year. One was hired locally; the other was invited in from out of town and was offered a job which he accepted.

Costs to hire:

Travel, meal and hotel expenses for 1 candidate:	$ 915.00
Share of cost of employment tests:	22.00
Medical exams and substance abuse screens (2 candidates)	240.00
Estimate of time of the personnel manager (35%) and of the personnel assistant (20%) involved in these two hires	18,400.00
	$19,577.00

Total estimated cost in the Personnel Dept. $19,577.00/2 hires = $9,788.50 per hire last year

Internal Progression/External Hiring

Some organizations are very interested in knowing to what degree they can promote from within, compared to the extent they must go outside of the company to fill openings. This percentage can be readily calculated as follows:

$$\frac{\text{\# Internal candidates promoted}}{\text{Total \# promotional opportunities}} \times 100 = \text{Internal promotion rate}$$

Similarly, a rate can be determined for the number of external hires.

Example: A mail order warehouse of 50 employees had ten promotional vacancies last year. Five of the vacancies were filled from present staff; the remainder were filled by outside hires. Therefore,

$$\frac{5}{10} \times 100[500 / 10] = 50\% \text{ Internal promotion rate}$$

In this example the external hire rate is also 50 percent.

Time Required to Fill a Position

Organizations with significant hiring activity often want to know how long it takes to fill a position. To develop this ratio, information is needed as follows:

- Date personnel office received the hire requisition
- Date new employee reported for work

The ratio is the time gap between starting a search and hiring a candidate.

$$\frac{\text{Total interval days}}{\text{Number of hires}} = \text{Hiring time}$$

Example: A customer service office had three hires last year, as follows:

- Customer service representative: Requisition January 2 and new employee reported for work February 2 (30 day interval).
- Receptionist: Requisition March 1 and new employee reported on the job March 18 (16 days).
- Customer service engineer: Vacancy occurred September 15th but decision to hire and requisition approved October 1; extensive interviewing then new hire reported to work December 10 (70 days).

To obtain the average number of days to fill a position:

$$\frac{30 + 16 + 70 = 116}{3} \, [116 \, / \, 3] = 39 \text{ days}$$

Benefits Costs Per Employee

Of high interest these days is the costs of benefits that companies provide to employees—both legally required and voluntarily provided by employers. Legally required benefits include employers' contributions to social security, unemployment compensation funds, workers compensation coverages, and other payroll taxes required by law. Voluntarily provided benefits can include costs of a medical insurance plan, dental or vision plans, pension or 401-K plans, cost of travel accident insurance, and the like.

Benefit costs can be determined as follows:

$$\frac{\text{Cost of all benefits}}{\text{Total payroll costs}} \times 100 = \text{Benefits as a \% of total payroll costs}$$

Example: A small customer service office of 4 employees had the following costs last year. Total payroll costs: $100,000; cost of all benefits: $36,000. Therefore,

$$\frac{\$36,000}{100,000} \times 100 \, [3,600,000 \, / \, 100,000] = 36\% \text{ benefit costs ratio to total payroll costs}$$

To determine the average benefits cost to the employer, divide $36,000 by 4 (employees) = $9,000

Hiring Rate of Interviews Held

How many interviews must be conducted before a job offer is made and accepted? Busy personnel staffs are anxious to have this kind of information so that they can fine-tune their selection and hiring procedures to make the process more productive.

A hiring rate for interviews conducted can be determined as follows:

$$\frac{\text{\# Hires last year}}{\text{\# Interviews conducted during the year}} = \text{Hiring rate}$$

Example: A rapidly expanding machine tool business tried to add more machinists last year and conducted extensive recruiting. Hundreds of resumes and applications were received from which a total of 72 interviews were conducted. Fifteen job offers were made and 12 new craft workers were hired. Therefore,

$$\frac{12}{72} = 16.7\% \text{ Hiring rate}$$

Injury Incidence Rate

Federal OSHA has set out a formula to determine the number of injuries, job illnesses, or lost workdays related to a common base of 100 full-time workers. It is presumed that each of these workers is employed for 50 weeks of the year, working 40 hours per week. The formula can be used to determine a number of accident indices, including:

▶ *Lost Workday Cases,* which involve days away from work or days of restricted work activity, or both

▶ *OSHA Recordable Cases,* which involve *all* work-related deaths and illnesses and those work-related injuries that result in loss of consciousness, restriction of work or motion, transfer to another job, or require medical treatment beyond first aid.

The formula is

$$\frac{\text{\# Injuries and / or job illnesses}}{\text{Total hours worked by all employees in the calendar year}} \times 200,000 = \text{Incidence rate}$$

Example: A manufacturing plant of 50 employees worked 100,000 hours last year. The plant incurred 5 lost work day cases (see definition above) in that year. Therefore,

$(5/100,000) \times 200,000 = $ Lost work day case rate of 10

The same plant had 20 OSHA recordable cases that required treatment at an outside medical facility. Therefore, the OSHA recordable case incidence rate is

$(20/100,000) \times 200,000 = $ OSHA recordable case incidence rate of 40

Workers' Compensation Costs

Costs of work injuries and illnesses as reflected in workers' compensation costs are of high interest to management. Excessive workers comp costs skim away company profits. Personnel managers will do well to review workers' comp cost trends regularly and give publicity to high costs or particular trends in costing.

Here are some methods to highlight workers' compensation costs.

Cost of workers compensation per employee:

$$\frac{\text{Total workers' comp costs in a given year}}{\text{Average \# employees in the year}} = \text{Average \$ costs of workers' comp per employee}$$

This calculation can be refined further to a cost in cents per hour for each hour worked.

Example: A manufacturing facility with 40 employees had $50,000 in workers compensation costs in a recent year. Therefore,

$$\frac{\$50,000}{40} = \$1,250 \text{ cost, on average, per employee}$$

Further example: Employees at this facility worked 80,000 hours last year. Therefore, the calculation can be further refined as,

$$\frac{\$50,000}{80,000} = \$0.625 \text{ cost of injuries per hour worked last year}$$

Appendix IV
Health and Safety Issues

Do small businesses need to be concerned about safety and job health of their workers? The answer clearly is "yes." Certainly, small organizations do not have the incidence of injuries or complex job health problems normally associated with larger organizations. And small organizations usually do not have the professional safety and health resources on staff typical of medium-sized or larger organizations.

But there are basic steps that can be taken by a small organization to establish a formal safety and health activity that will reduce accidents and control workers' compensation costs.

In the small organization a line manager, a respected supervisor or the personnel manager may be asked to "set up a safety program."

That task can be made easier and the safety program can be more focused and effective if management raises the following questions within its own staff group *before* embarking on a formal safety activity:

What Are the Safety Hazards in this Business?

An early step in developing a formal safety activity is to determine the depth and breadth of hazards in the operation. Hazard identification can help make the workplace physically safe and occupationally healthy by minimizing injuries from equipment and developing safe work procedures to protect employees on the job.

Hazards vary from company to company and industry to industry. Workers in a small office, for example, usually have few hazard exposures—the tripping dangers of an extended electrical cord from a typewriter or word processor. Word processing operators may develop soreness in their hands and wrists, potentially the beginning of cumulative trauma disorders such as carpal tunnel syndrome.

In a warehousing operation, for instance, fork lift trucks may be the principal hazard (that is, the danger from the toppling of unsteady loads of finished goods).

Hazards in a manufacturing setting are usually significantly greater—machinery hazards in the production process, possibly toxic chemicals, electrical dangers, fire hazards, and the like. On a construction site hazard potential is even more severe—falls, electrical dangers, and hazards from hand tools and other construction machinery.

Accident and occupational illness records should also provide an indication of the significance of the problem. Review of the first aid log for a year will show whether minor, incidental injuries are occurring or whether there are major trauma injuries at the work site.

Time spent identifying the hazards inherent in the operation, then focusing on corrective measures are important first steps to shaping a successful safety activity.

What Are the Costs of Accidents?

Business managers need to know the costs of accidents and on-the-job illnesses. A review of workers' compensation, monthly, quarterly or annual cost printouts will provide bottom line determinations of the extent of the problem. Low or token accident costs may indicate the need for a minimal safety activity; higher accident costs may require a broader, formal safety program.

Is the Company in Compliance with Basic Safety Laws and Regulations?

Any company in manufacturing, distribution, longshoring and maritime, agriculture, or construction has a legal obligation to meet federal or state OSHA Act requirements, standards, regulations, and guidelines. A schedule of fines is provided for those organizations found to be out of compliance with OSHA regulations.

Federal OSHA directs employers under its General Duty Clause of the OSH Act in Section 5(a)(1) to provide "Employment and a place of employment which is free from recognized hazards that are causing or are likely to cause death or serious physical harm." The benefits of a safe and healthful workplace are quickly translated into improved employee morale and increased productivity.

What Are the Objectives of a Safety Activity?

Is it your management objective to provide a safe and healthy work environment for employees? Is your objective to reduce workers' compensation costs and other losses caused by accidents? That objective is a popular one and likely to attract interest and attention from senior management.

Is your management objective to eliminate further "harassment" by OSHA inspectors? An effective safety and health program that targets OSHA compliance as an early objective will accomplish that goal and be putting many of the elements of an effective safety program in place at the same time.

Management needs to focus on one or more of these objectives as the thrust of their formal safety activity.

What Are the Priorities?

The accident history of the facility should dictate the first priorities of a safety program. Other formal safety activities can come later but high-cost or serious problems should be attacked first.

A company with a high level of machinery injuries should put this first in their attack on accidents and a leading ingredient of their safety inspection and audit program. An organization with a history of nagging dermatitis problems would logically call in an industrial hygienist and occupational dermatologist for assistance in the effort to control skin infections on the job. A series of injuries involving fork lift trucks should involve an examination of lift-truck maintenance procedures, driver training, pedestrian precautions and the like.

Who Will Be Responsible for the Safety Program?

Some companies assign a safety manager, the human resources manager, or the plant nurse responsibility for the local safety program. These staff persons can assist greatly in the development and implementation of the program but are not likely to make it effective.

Responsibility and accountability for an effective safety and health program must be with the appropriate line manager responsible for the operation—the company president in the case of a small business, the plant manager, the distribution center supervisor, or the office manager in a satellite office.

Safety, medical, and human resources staff can assist greatly but leadership must come from the ranking line manager so that the objectives of the program can be carried through the levels of supervision and to the employees themselves.

Are Basic First Aid Facilities in Place?

Even the smallest organizations should have a first-aid cabinet and supplies. Depending on the extent of the risks or hazards, the size of your employee group, and the typical type of injury, trained first aiders should be on staff.

Training is key in an effective first-aid and medical service. First-aid attendants should be trained by professional organizations specializing in industrial first-aid training. Occupational health personnel either on staff or on retainer should know the facility, the risks or exposures, and easy entry and exit pathways.

Is Top Management Really Committed to a Formal Safety and Health Activity?

The cornerstone of success of a safety program is management commitment to support the activity. That commitment is usually easier to obtain in a small organization when management understands the objectives of the program—what type of safety activity will take place, what the objectives of the program are, what costs are involved, what costs are expected to come within greater control as a result of a more formal safety activity.

The most effective forms of management commitment are personal leadership by executives, key managers and supervisors, approval of expenditures, and follow up on the effectiveness of the program.

Will Employees Be Involved in the Safety Program?

Organizations successful with their safety programs and loss-control activities invariably point to employee involvement as a key ingredient of that activity. Most employees are conscious of the safety hazards of their jobs and how to perform the job safely. Alert organizations tap these resources through activities such as safety committees, safety inspection tours, and other employee input to the safety awareness process. Employee involvement in the safety program is a natural for a small business where people know one another well and there is a high personal interest in protecting the safety of co-workers.

A safety committee can help maintain active, positive interest in safety among co-workers and provide recommendations and advice to management to correct hazards and focus on unsafe work habits. Safety committees usually have representation from each department or major organizational unit and meet at least monthly to review safety activities—any serious injuries, results of safety inspections, progress toward goals, safety hazards, unsafe work practices, and the like. A prearranged agenda, compulsory attendance at the meetings, and education and training films and videos are essential to making this activity effective. A safety committee, actively supported by a management that acts on the committee's logical recommendations can provide considerable assistance in solving safety and health problems.

Will Safety Inspections or Audits Be Conducted?

A list of hazards and unsafe work practices can readily become the basis for safety audit inspection forms, the report card on how well a facility is doing in controlling hazards and monitoring work practices.

By department, work area, or specific machine a listing can be made of unsafe conditions and unsafe acts encountered in the analysis process. Safety inspection tours, using supervisors, safety committee members, and regular employees will then have specific direction to their auditing activities, much better than a blank piece of paper and a clipboard to take notes as they roam around on their inspection tours.

Like any business activity, safety audits need a follow-up mechanism to provide a feeling of assurance that the unsafe conditions have, in fact, been corrected and any unsafe acts observed have been reported and employees retrained in the correct work procedures.

Will New and Transferred Employees Be Trained in Safe Work Practices?

New hires and employees transferred to new jobs in the facility should be trained in the hazards and safe work practices of their jobs.

A safety training checklist can be readily developed to accomplish this training and provide the supervisor or job trainer with an excellent way to see that critical safety points have been covered.

Will Accidents Be Investigated—Really Investigated?

If an accident should occur, who has the responsibility to investigate the incident? Organizations with effective safety programs assign that responsibility initially to the immediate supervisor with overview of the results by management and, in some cases, by the safety committee. Too often, though, especially in small organizations with informal procedures, a cursory investigation is conducted and a written report may or may not be made of the incident.

An accident reporting questionnaire should ask questions in depth about what happened, the employee's statement of what happened, the supervisor's statement of what happened and then, perhaps most important, what corrective actions are to be taken by whom, in what time frame, to correct the situation and prevent recurrence.

How Will Safety Be Communicated to Employees?

A successful safety program will bring out good things about the company and its employees. Those successes should be told to the employees, their families, and to the community.

Communications of any kind is easier to handle in the small organization—word-of-mouth communications can be used easily. But there are supplemental materials that managers and supervisors can use to get the message across—media such as newsletters, letters to the home, safety displays in the facility, prominent posting of safety committee minutes, and display of safety awards can all add to positive communications about successful safety activities.

Answers to these questions can help shape a safety activity for a small facility that is cost effective and directed to attacking its hazardous exposures and unsafe work practices.

Appendix V
Resources to Help

BOOKS

Employee Benefits Compliance Made Simple, from Business and Legal Reports, 39 Academy St., Madison, Connecticut 06443.

Information to comply with latest employee benefit regulations. Also from the same publisher, *The Job Description Encyclopedia*, which contains dozens of sample job descriptions and the techniques of how to write job descriptions and keep them current.

Encyclopedia of Prewritten Personnel Policies, from Business and Legal Reports Inc., Madison, Connecticut 06443.

An outstanding and helpful work of generic personnel policies on everything from absenteeism through workers' compensation.

The Federal Wage and Hour Laws, by Brian Dixon, 1994, The Society for Human Resource Management, 606 N. Washington St., Alexandria, Virginia 22314.

Guide to Employee Handbooks, by Robert J. Nobile. Warren Gorham and Lamont, Boston.

An excellent guide to the development of employee handbooks by a leading lawyer-writer in the field.

Leadership Skills: Standout Performance for Human Resource Managers by William R. Tracey, AMACOM Books, New York.

A four-part plan to hone personnel management skills, business/financial skills, people skills, and technical skills.

A Manager's Guide to OSHA, by Neville C. Tompkins, Crisp Publications, 1200 Hamilton Court, Menlo Park, California 94025.

Explains employer and employee rights under the federal OSH Act and tells how to effectively manage an OSHA inspection.

The Right to Understand: Linking Literacy to Health and Safety Training, Michelle Gonzalez Arroyo and Betty Szudy, Labor Occupational Health Program, University of California Berkeley.

The last chapter contains recommendations for employers to help overcome literacy problems in safety and health. LOHP Publications, 2514 Channing Way, Berkeley, California 94720.

Training Methods That Work, Lois B. Hart, Ed.d, Crisp Publications, Inc., Menlo Park, California.

Turning Your Human Resources Department into a Profit Center, by Michael W. Mercer, AMACOM Books, New York.

The purpose of business is to make a profit and the author gives lively examples of how to turn routine personnel assignments into valuable business activities.

OTHER PUBLICATIONS

The Annual SHRM-CCH Survey (Society for Human Resource Management/Commerce Clearing House, Inc.)

Defines HR practices that contribute to bottom-line success. The 10th annual survey was conducted in 1995 and a copy is available from CCH, Inc., 4025 W. Peterson Ave., Chicago, Illinois 60646.

Business and Legal Reports Inc., 39 Academy St., Madison, Connecticut 06443.

Publishes a number of publications in human resource management, safety and health, and environmental affairs.

HR Magazine, published by the Society for Human Resource Management, 606 N. Washington St., Alexandria, Virginia 22314.

Human Resource Manager's Legal Reporter, Ransome and Benjamin Publishers, 14 Highview Avenue, Old Greenwich, Connecticut 06870.

A monthly newsletter that reports on legal developments affecting human resources. Also publishes *Job Safety Consultant.*

Human Resources Effectiveness Report, The Saratoga Institute, 12950 Saratoga Avenue, Saratoga, California 95070.

An annual survey of the cost and value of various human resource activities.

Personnel Journal published by ACC Communications, Inc., 245 Fischer Ave., Costa Mesa, California 92626.

Bureau of National Affairs, P.O. Box 6036, Rockville, Maryland 20850.
Offers a wide variety of publications and daily, weekly, and monthly releases on changes in government laws and regulations.

London House, 1550 Northwest Highway, Park Ridge, Illinois 60068.
A major publisher of honesty and personality tests.

GOVERNMENT PUBLICATIONS

Americans with Disabilities Act and the EEOC *Technical Assistance Manual* (for the ADA).
Single copies available from Equal Employment Opportunity Commission, 1801 L St., NW, Washington D.C. 20507.

General Industry Digest, a summary of federal OSHA regulations applicable to plants and offices in general industry, available from the local OSHA area office listed under "United States Government," in the blue pages of the local telephone book.

Guide to Record Retention Requirements, available from the federal Superintendent of Documents, Washington D.C. 20402.

Uniform Guidelines on Employee Selection Procedures, from the federal Equal Employment Opportunity Commission, 1978. The guidelines provide information on procedures to ensure that a test is reliable and valid.

SOFTWARE

Low-Cost Human Resources Software, from HR Press, 9119 Skinner Road, Fredonia, New York 14063. Includes a wide range of low-cost human resource software, including employee record-keeping systems and applicant tracking.

The SHRM Learning System, six modules in human resource management, the study of which prepares a person for writing human resource certification examinations. The modules cover management practices, selection and placement, employee and labor relations, compensation and benefits, training and development, health safety and security, and international human resources management. Interactive computer disks are provided for this workbook and self-teaching system. Details and costs from SHRM Distribution Center, 1600 West 82nd St., Minneapolis, Minnesota 55431 (800) 444-5006.

ORGANIZATIONS

American Compensation Association, 14040 N. Northsight Blvd., Scottsdale Arizona 85260.

The professional association of compensation managers. The Association has recently published a booklet "Compensation Basics for HR Generalists," one of a series. Also offers information on managerial and employee incentive plans.

American Society for Training and Development, 1630 Duke St., Alexandria, Virginia 22313.

The professional association for employer-based trainers.

College Placement Council, 62 Highland Ave., Bethlehem, Pennsylvania 18017.

National professional institution that provides communication and interaction between institutions of higher education and employers of college graduates.

Employee Assistance Professionals Association, 4601 North Fairfax Drive, Arlington, Virginia 22203.

Organization of employee assistance professionals. Can refer employers to EAP facilities in their area.

Employment Management Association, 4101 Lake Boone Trail, Raleigh, North Carolina 27607.

The professional association for persons who specialize in recruitment and placement activities.

G. Neil Companies, 720 International Parkway, Sunrise, Florida 33345 and *HR Direct,* 100 Enterprise Place, Dover, Delaware 19901.

Provides standard personnel forms and human resources software.

Human Resource Systems Professionals, P.O. Box 801646, Dallas, Texas 75380.

The organization for professionals who work with human resource information systems.

Human Resource Certification Institute, 606 North Washington St., Alexandria, Virginia 22314. (703) 548-3440.

The professional certification institute in human resources management.

International Society of Certified Employee Benefits Specialists, 18700 W. Bluemound Rd., Brookfield, Wisconsin 53008.

Organization for professionals in the field of employee benefits.

National Safety Council, 1121 Spring Lake Drive, Itasca, Illinois 60143.

The international not-for-profit organization in workplace safety and health.

National Safety Management Society, 12 Pickens Lane, Weaverville, North Carolina 28787.

Membership is open to anyone with responsibilities in safety and loss control.

The President's Committee on Employment of Individuals with Disabilities, 1331 F Street, N.W., Washington D.C. 20004. (202) 376-6200 voice or (202) 376-6205 TDD.

A national coordinating agency to enhance employment of persons with disabilities.

Society for Human Resource Management, SHRM is headquartered at 606 North Washington St., Alexandria, Virginia 22314. For information on membership, conferences, and seminars call (800) 283-7476.

SHRM is the leading organization of the human resources profession, representing nearly 70,000 professionals and student members worldwide. SHRM provides educational and information services, conferences and seminars, government representation and publications, including *HR Magazine* and *HR News.* SHRM has membership chapters throughout the country.

ABOUT THE AUTHOR

Neville C. Tompkins, of Cedar Run, New Jersey, is a human resources consultant and writer whose consulting activities focus on assisting small businesses with their personnel management problems and programs.

He was formerly a Director of Human Resources at the corporate offices of Continental Can Co., Inc., and since 1989, has offered human resources consulting assistance to small businesses. He has achieved the Senior Professional in Human Resources (SPHR) status, the highest level of professional certification in the profession.

He is the author of a number of books in the human resources field, including *How to Write an Affirmative Action Plan* (Business and Legal Reports, Inc.). He has also written several books in the safety and occupational health field, including *A Manager's Guide to OSHA* (Crisp Publications, Inc.).